Readin' Writin' & Route 21

A Pictorial History of an American Road

by Robert A. Musson, M.D.

Copyright 2010 by the author
Created by Zepp Publications, Medina, Ohio, USA
contact: grossvater@zoominternet.net

ISBN #978-0-9668954-3-8

Library of Congress Control Number: 2010936840

Cover art created by the author

Printing and binding done by Docucopies.com

TABLE OF CONTENTS

ACKNOWLEDGEMENTS

This project has been many years in the making, as I have gathered information and images from a variety of sources, mostly a combination of personal photos from my travels or postcards and maps acquired through the eBay website. I certainly wish to thank Kevin Wise, the late Mike Kirschner, and Tim Murphy for tolerating my obsession with following this road, as well as my parents, Irv and Fritz Musson, who unwittingly introduced me to it more than forty years ago, and my wife Jennifer who has traveled on portions of the road with me in recent years despite her tendency toward motion sickness on the curvier sections.

The website www.wikipedia.org has been a vital source of obscure information on a variety of subjects related to Route 21 and sites along its course. A book of this type is much easier to produce with accessibility to information via the internet in this era.

I would also like to thank Michael Roberson and his websites chronicling the highways of Virginia and the Carolinas for his expert help on tracking the many changes in alignment of Route 21 over the years. His knowledge and access to vintage road maps has made a dramatic difference in the degree of accuracy in the information presented in this book.

Thanks also goes to Fred Miller of the Tuscarawas County Historical Society for information and some great images of Dover and New Philadelphia, Ohio.

Thanks to Theresa Hart, writer of an article in the *Wytheville Enterprise* on February 21, 2003, and Ralph Berrier, Jr., writer of a similar article in the *Roanoke Times* on October 17, 2009.

Thanks also goes to the following for their assistance: John Dodson of the Bland County Historical Archives; John M. Hudson; Karen Stuebing; Michael Hale; Sy Commanday; www.newrivernotes.com; Jerry Fuhrman; Levente Jakab; and Michael Summa.

I hope I have covered everyone who has been of assistance, and I apologize for anyone who was inadvertently left off the list.

INTRODUCTION

U.S. Route 21 was born in November 1926 when the federal government established the U.S. Highway System as a series of numbered routes that would eventually connect all of the country's major cities with improved roads for travel and commerce. Prior to that time, there had been a vague network of auto trails, which were named roads (such as the Lincoln Highway) that covered long stretches, usually across several states or in some cases across the entire country. In addition, there were numerous local roads, some of which had numbers assigned to them, and most of these were either improved versions of old stage coach lines going back a century or more, or were roads built parallel to existing railroads, rivers, or canals, where a right-of-way was already established.

Once the new numbered routes were established, the roads were generally improved (meaning graded and in most cases paved), except in some of the most remote areas of the country, and shield-shaped white signs, sixteen inches in diameter, were placed accordingly to guide travelers from one town to another. Although coordinated by the federal government, the U.S. Highway System has always been maintained by the individual states in which the roads lie. Eventually, all of the roads would be paved, and many were improved from winding two lane country roads to four-lane divided highways, often bypassing the towns and cities that they were originally meant to link. Development of the U.S. Highway System continued into the 1950s, when the newer, national Interstate system became a higher priority and began to replace some of the older routes.

Outline of the modern-day U.S. Highway System as of 2009

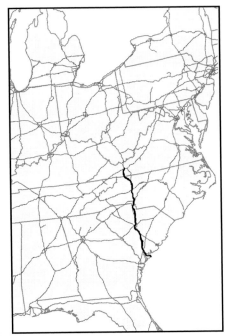

When the new national highway system was put into use, it primarily utilized existing roads and combined local routes, state routes, or longer named auto trails to cover a given territory. The numbering system generally used odd numbers for north-south roads, and even numbers for east-west roads. When Route 21 was established, it was considered to be one of the primary north-south highways, linking Cleveland, Ohio and Lake Erie with the Atlantic Ocean in the south. It sometime went by the name of "Great Lakes to Florida Highway"; the original planned version of 21 had it continuing south to Jacksonville, FL., although in its final version, the route would end in South Carolina, 180 miles to the north. While the road was established on paper in 1926, various sections had not yet been constructed, particularly in the more isolated and mountainous parts of West Virginia and Virginia. Instead of using older, treacherous, unsafe roads over mountains, certain segments of the new Federal Route were not completed and marked with signs until 1927 or even 1928, with longer, inconvenient, temporary detour routes used in the mean time.

While the new road dramatically helped to improve travel through Appalachia and the South, it had a particular significance in linking Ohio and West Virginia, a link that continues to this day. By the 1920s, the rubber boom had begun in Akron, and along with a growing steel industry in Cleveland, Canton, and Youngstown, Northeast Ohio looked very appealing to West Virginians who lived in areas where coal mining or farming was not as fruitful as it had once been. Over the next thirty years, a large and steady influx of Mountain State residents came north for jobs, and in most cases, they traveled on the one main highway that connected the two regions: Route 21.

Although West Virginians went all over Ohio to work, a large proportion of them went to the Rubber Capital of the World, working at Goodyear, Goodrich, Firestone, etc. At one point during the Great Depression, nearly ten percent of Akron's population was made up of people from West Virginia, leading to one common joke that the capital of West Virginia was Akron. The city was such a popular destination for several reasons; the simplest reason was that it was closer to home than Cleveland, making it easier to travel back to see family. In addition, the rubber companies themselves recruited workers from West Virginia, seeing them as strong workers who could handle the heavy labor involved in tire making. There was also a feeling among tire makers that workers from the south would have a more independent spirit than European immigrants that were also competing for jobs, and would be less inclined to be influenced by union organizers and worse yet, communists.

Initially, many of them would work in Akron during the week and travel back home on the weekend, making Route 21 a very busy road in both directions. It was the heavy use of this road that led to another common joke that the three R's in West Virginia schools were Readin', Ritin', and Route 21 to Akron (similarly, Columbus residents often joked that the three R's in Kentucky schools were Readin', Ritin', and Route 23 to Columbus). Eventually, many of them stayed in Akron to build new lives, and many of their descendants remain there today. For a more in-depth picture of the Appalachian migration to Akron's rubber factories, I highly recommend

Wheels of Fortune: The Story of Rubber in Akron, by Steve Love and David Giffels.

Looking Down Route 21 and 52, showing South Bluefield, W. Va.

Postcard view looking down on Bluefield from East River Mountain in the daylight

And now for the personal side of the road...my interest in Route 21 began in November 1969, at the age of six, while returning home from a family vacation in Florida. At the time, 21 was the primary highway connecting the Carolinas with our home in Northeast Ohio, as the interstate system was still under construction. On the last night of our trip, my parents and I were traveling north on the road, having left Columbia, S.C. earlier in the day. By nightfall, we had just climbed into the mountains of northern North Carolina and western Virginia, with a destination of Bluefield, WV. In the darkness, the road seemed far more isolated than it had during the day, challenging my father to maneuver our 1965 Pontiac LeMans along the endless curves and hills.

The part that stayed in my memory most vividly was the section of 21 north of Wytheville, VA., as we began to traverse the most mountainous stretch of the entire route. A long series of tight, hairpin turns took us first up to the top of Big Walker Mountain, the highest point along the road, and then immediately down the other side. Several miles later we went through the sleepy villages of Bland and Bastian, crossing a slightly less intimidating Brushy Mountain along the way. For the next several miles we drove through the valley of Wolf Creek, which we crossed several times along the winding road before reaching the village of Rocky Gap. Along the way were billboards advertising the motels and restaurants of Bluefield, which seemed like it must be a mountain oasis, as we had scarcely seen a single business since leaving Wytheville nearly an hour earlier.

After passing Rocky Gap, we began another long ascent with a series of tight curves which took us to the top of East River Mountain, which marks the state line separating the Virginias. From there we could see the twinkling lights of the south side of Bluefield, where the previously advertised motels beckoned for us to visit. Descending the north side of the mountain, we quickly found ourselves at our destination, where we checked in at the Highlander Motel for the night. The next morning, the room's black and white television had nothing but religious programming on the three available channels, reminding us that we were still in the Bible Belt. We left for home soon after that, taking the mostly completed but far less exciting Interstate 77 most of the way back to Akron.

Something about the drive that evening was particularly fascinating to my six-year-old eyes and stayed with me for years. To this day I'm not exactly sure why, but I imagine it was a combination of the mountainous terrain, which was certainly unlike

Postcard from the Brier Motel in Bluefield, WV.; by 1969 it had been renamed as the Highlander Motel and today it remains in business as a low-budget Economy Inn.

anything we had ever encountered in Ohio, and the quaint villages we had passed through along the way. I was also intrigued by the concept that we were traveling on the same Route 21 that went near our home as Cleveland-Massillon Road, albeit several hundred miles away. Somehow my small world became a little bit larger that night.

Fast forward to 1983, which was the next time that we traveled through the same area while on a trip to the ocean in South Carolina. While traveling home, the memory of the earlier trip came back to me when I saw signs for Route 21 in Virginia, and while I would have been happy to exit there and travel the old road back home, or at least through the mountainous areas, my father was only interested in getting home in the straightest and fastest way possible, which meant I-77 the whole way back. Two years later, however, I would finally get my chance to cover the entire route at one time. What I would find out in the process, however, was that U.S. Route 21 no longer existed in Ohio, the road's northern half having lost its national highway designation in 1971; its only relic in our area was a section known as state Route 21. This was a common occurence, with many U.S highways having come and gone and been rerouted over the years; U.S. Route 25 in western Ohio, running parallel to Interstate 75 between Toledo and Cincinnati, was also decommissioned and now begins in northern Kentucky.

In the summer of 1985, I had just graduated from college and was getting ready to leave home and move to Columbus to start medical school. During the four month layoff, I had time to relax and enjoy the summer for a change, and many evenings were spent driving around aimlessly with my friends Kevin and Mike. A good deal of Northeast Ohio was covered on those drives, and although we were painfully "clean" kids, with no smoking, drinking, or drug use going on, the conversations were endlessly entertaining with sarcasm and laughs aplenty. While the others would have generally been content to sit on the front porch and watch cars go by while talking, I was the one who seemed to have that need to drive around and see the "sights" of the area. As a result, I was the one who was always driving them about in my powder blue

1975 Pontiac Bonneville, a beast of a car that my father often referred to as the Queen Mary. Despite the car getting about ten miles to the gallon, gas wasn't terribly expensive in those days and all in all driving around like this was pretty cheap entertainment.

On one of our drives that summer, we had an occasion to take Cleveland-Massillon Road (known as "Old 21" in the area) north toward Cleveland when Mike asked (innocently enough), "where does this road end?" Never one to let a question like that go unanswered, and in the days when Mapquest wasn't available to answer such a question in mere seconds, I proceeded to drive them north to Cleveland on Old 21, giving us all the answer. Several nights later, we were back on the road for another cruise, this time going south. Not surprisingly, the same question came up again, but this time the answer wasn't quite so easy. I knew the road more or less

56 SOLDIERS' AND SAILORS' MONUMENT, PUBLIC SQUARE,

THE STANDARD BUILDING

CLEVELAND, OHIO   4A-H1665

Public Square in Cleveland; the actual northern end of 21 was directly behind the monument in this picture, at the intersection of Ontario Street and Superior Avenue.

continued several states to the south, but I knew none of the details involved in getting there. I don't remember which one of us came up with the idea that night, but with nothing but our low-paying busboy jobs at local restaurants holding us back, the concept of traveling the entire length of Route 21 was born.

Several weeks later, once we could collectively schedule time to get away, we made our plans to actually do it: travel the entire length of 21! Looking at a current road atlas, I quickly realized that 21 no longer existed in Ohio or West Virginia, so that following the old road would be a real challenge with no signs marking the road and no maps to rely on. Over the next few weeks, I managed to find two Ohio road maps from the 1950s at a local flea market (easily finding such things on eBay was still years away), which would turn out to be a vital part of making the trip work. On a Monday morning in late August, we set off on our journey, planning to leave early with a first-night destination of Bluefield, WV. Despite having some doubts about the intelligence of undertaking this adventure, I made motel reservations that morning, packed, and headed out. Being a purist even at the age of 22, I had one condition for this voyage: we would start at the very beginning of the route, and follow the entire road to its end point. Mike and Kevin didn't seem to care too much either way, as their primary interest was getting to swim in the ocean at the end of the trip, which the maps indicated would be at Fripp Island, SC. Clearly they had underestimated just how long it would take to drive the whole length of 21. I had one other goal of this trip: to somehow bring back a Route 21 sign to hang on my wall. Clearly I had underestimated how difficult (and illegal) that would be and ultimately how long it would take for me to get one.

We started with a half-hour drive to Cleveland, where the trip would start at Public Square around 9 a.m. Kevin was sitting in the passenger seat, as he would for the next five days, keeping a log of every town or significant sight we encountered as well as the time and mileage at each of these points. It was his suggestion that we put a sign on the back of the car saying "Fripp Island or bust," but surprisingly I wasn't looking to draw attention to our endeavor at the time. Now, while I like to think that I'm not particularly superstitious, literally as we were crossing the square, which technically was to be the start of the trip, a spider came down from the ceiling and landed on my shoulder. It wasn't a large one, but with a decent case of arachnophobia that I deal with, it certainly got my attention before being brushed away. Within seconds of that, we were a block away from the square when steam began to billow out from under the car's hood. I'm no automobile expert, but even I knew this was not a good sign, especially on a ten-year-old car.

Immediately figuring that the trip was cursed, I pulled over several blocks away, once we were out of the major traffic lanes. Mike and Kevin looked under the hood and made a quick diagnosis: a blown radiator hose, something that would be relatively easy to fix. We found a car parts store two miles down the road, and within fifteen minutes they had the hose replaced and the leak had been fixed. The next stop was the nearest Burger King, as it had already gotten to be late morning and the boys were hungry, not to mention dirty from the repair job. As they exited the men's room after a lengthy cleaning up, Kevin muttered to Mike "Are you clean up to your

SCENE ON OHIO RIVER, MARIETTA, OHIO

Crossing the Ohio River near Marietta, the original Williamstown Bridge was an oddly asymmetric structure, built in 1903 and demolished in 1987.

elbows?" A healthy dose of wry humor kept the mood light throughout the trip, as it would turn out. Once we left the restaurant, I decided that this first leg of the trip hadn't gone too well, so we should start again from scratch. We went back to Public Square, and at 11:29 a.m. the journey officially began.

Now came the tough part–finding our way along Old 21. The maps were reasonably good guides and we soon found our way out of Cleveland and headed south. As we passed through the western suburbs of Akron, a short distance from our homes, I sheepishly looked at the clock: 12:26 p.m. We had spent the entire morning just getting back to where we had started, and at this point came my first realization that our first night's destination might not work out.

County after county passed as well as many intersections with Interstate 77, 21's modern-day replacement. While 77 was visible from many sections of 21, we encountered several lengthy stretches of 21 in southern Ohio that were far from the interstate. More than one of those stretches seemed very isolated, leading to questions as to whether we were still on the right road, until we finally found ourselves in Marietta at the Ohio River just past 5 p.m. The obvious way across, however, was not so obvious on this day...the aging bridge across the river had closed to all traffic just a month earlier (permanently, it turned out, as the bridge was demolished soon after that and rebuilt on the same site). Detouring to the I-77 bridge two miles east, we entered West Virginia and quickly got back to old 21, continuing through Parkersburg and points south.

Driving along more and more curves and hills, we slowly wound our way toward Charleston, watching the shadows getting longer all the time. It was nearly dark when we reached the state capitol, and the realization hit that we would get no further on this first day. Finding a low-budget Knight's Inn across the river (and sadly not on 21), we checked in around 10 pm. We

were disappointed to find the motel pool closed, so we headed across the street for a late dinner at a Rax restaurant. The long day left all of us tired, and even after a decent night's sleep (although I awoke at 4 a.m. to see Mike sitting at the end of the bed watching cartoons on the TV since he was having trouble staying asleep), nobody was in a hurry to get up the next morning. Leaving the motel at 11:30, we found our way back to 21 and continued along the Kanawha River through Boomer, Smithers, and Gauley Bridge before ascending the first long, steep, winding hill. This gave us a nice view at the top before descending immediately to cross the river and continue through Fayetteville, Oak

(top right) The Queen Mary ascending East River Mountain on Old 21 in 1985. To this day I have no idea how or why this photo was taken. The entire mountain road was a series of tight curves like this one; (right) Abandoned gas station in Rocky Gap, VA., near the base of the mountain.

Despite the haze, the view from Big Walker Mountain was worth the drive up there.

Hill, Beckley, Spanishburg, Princeton, and finally by mid-afternoon, Bluefield. By this time it was a miracle that we weren't all severely carsick.

After a quick lunch, we got onto U.S. Route 52, which had at one time shared the road with 21, and went through the East River Mountain tunnel and into Virginia. At the time I didn't realize that this was not the original road, which in fact went all the way up and over the mountain (as I had done in 1969) instead of through it. I would figure that out on the return trip, thus realizing that we hadn't actually traveled the entire trip on Old 21. Still, I thought we were doing a pretty good job considering the situation. Entering Virginia, I considered the next hour or two the true "heart" of 21, and it was the section that had fascinated me so much as a child. High mountains (by Appalachian standards) and small villages in the valleys were plentiful in this area, although it looked a lot different in the daytime than it had at night. Another long series of tight curves took us up Big Walker Mountain, where we stopped at the lookout tower and store. With a healthy fear of heights, I chose not to climb to the top of the 100 foot tower, but the ground level view was only slightly less spectacular. After leaving and heading down the mountain, we continued on to Wytheville.

Once in Wytheville, we saw for the first time, one of my personal goals for the trip: a true Route 21 sign! In recent years, the 21 designation had been removed from the northern half of the road, but it still existed from Wytheville south, and from here on the signs would be common sight. Most were the standard 24 inch square signs shown at the right, but we also saw smaller shield-shaped signs (below) in some of the more rural areas. I later learned that the smaller signs were a remnant of the past and were unique to Virginia. I immediately began to think of ways to get a sign to take home, and once we had reached a particularly isolated section of the road, we decided to make a try for one. Pulling over to the side of the road, I opened the hood of the car as an excuse, and while Kevin and I pretended to be looking at the engine for the source of a supposed noise it was making, Mike made an attempt to pull down a nearby sign. Only then did we realize how tightly those signs were bolted into place, and how our small wrench was overmatched. When the bolts wouldn't even budge, we tried pulling the post out of the ground altogether, although the state department of trans-

portation had apparently been prepared for our shenanigans, and the concrete base of the post was not about to move anywhere. Another try further down the road left us with similar results, and the quest for a sign had quickly come to an end. Only in more recent years, thanks to eBay, was I able to find two 21 signs, one of each type, from dealers who had the foresight to go to the state's scrapyard, where retired signs were available if you showed up at the right time.

Despite the sign fiasco, we continued into North Carolina, where the hills and curves gradually became less severe as we got away from the mountains. At that point we encountered the first rain of the trip, which would continue well into the night. After arriving at our Red Roof Inn in Statesville, a major thunderstorm provided some entertainment before going to bed. The next morning, we again slept in and didn't check out until around 11. Once on the road again, we weren't out of the city before a familiar smell entered the car: antifreeze, followed by the sight of steam coming out of the hood yet again. Finding the nearest parts store, we found a leak in a different section of radiator hose, which was again fixed in short order so that we could continue our trip. At this point we realized that we had arrived in the South, as the heat and humidity were fairly intense outside the car. Continuing on our way, we eventually reached Charlotte, where 21 had been rerouted onto I-77 bypassing the city, and finding the exact original route was challenging. Using the old map, we did well through the city until getting a little confused on the south end, but eventually we found our way into South Carolina, the last of the five states on our journey.

Going through Fort Mill, SC, I noticed two old shield-shaped 21 signs along the road that

appeared to have been from the 1950s. The oldest signs that we found along the entire route, somehow they had survived all these years. Again, my first instinct was to somehow figure a way to get one of them as a souvenir, but with nowhere to pull over and being in a residential area in the light of day, I decided against making another attempt to remove one. In later years, however, return trips showed that the old signs were eventually replaced, and to this day I've never seen a 21 sign like it for sale anywhere.

After passing through Rock Hill, SC, the road became extremely isolated, with little scenery for more than an hour before reaching the state capital in Columbia. After lunch here, we continued out of the city and onward through the countryside toward the ocean. Soon after that came our first viewing of spanish moss hanging from the trees, telling us that we were definitely getting closer to the end. More rain showers rolled into the region, and the last fifty miles of the drive were through drizzle as we approached the town of Beaufort, where we checked in at the local Holiday Inn, our one big splurge for the trip. Having traveled so far, however, I didn't feel like stopping just twenty miles or so from the end of 21. So despite the complaints of the others, we piled back into the car and continued through the pitch black darkness from one island to another, as scattered flashes of lightning danced around in the sky. Finally we reached Hunting Island, where the reflective paint of a particular sign loomed in the distance: "End 21". We had finally reached it! In the darkness it wasn't really a photo opportunity, so the end really wasn't as exciting as I had hoped. We turned around and went back to the hotel for the night.

Setting out the next morning, the sun had returned as we traveled back out through the low country, crossing several bridges over coastal inlets and rivers before returning to the End 21 sign.

This was definitely a photo opportunity, and I posed next to the sign as if I had actually accomplished something. In retrospect I had set a goal and had followed through with it, and 850 miles or so later, nobody had gotten hurt and no laws were broken (despite our attempts), so I had to consider it a successful trip overall. Although 21 officially ended at Hunting Island State

Swing bridge along Route 21, connecting St. Helena Island and Harbor Island, SC.; here it is in action, stopping traffic to let a fishing boat go by in August 1985.

Park, the road continued south a few more miles to Fripp Island, so we continued a little further until reaching the gate at the entrance to the island, at which time we were told in no uncertain terms that the island was private and we would have to turn around. No problem, as we went back to Hunting Island, where a beautiful public beach awaited us. Spending some time in the ocean waves seemed like a nice reward for a trip well done, despite an apparent attack of sand fleas, which we figured out that night when all of us started itching. After a couple hours at the beach, we realized it was time to head home. This time, the return trip north was entirely via interstate highways, and it took just a day and a half, exactly half the time that the trip south had taken on 21.

Two weeks after returning home, I moved to Columbus to start medical school at Ohio State, and that fact put an exclamation point on the 21 trip. In a lot of ways, it was a coda for my youth, as adulthood and all of its responsibilities lay ahead. But for more than two decades since that time, I have often thought back to those five days in August 1985, when I felt like I didn't have a care in the world aside from making sure we were on the right road. Nowadays I honestly can't believe that such a time ever existed in my life!

I would return to 21 several times in the future, driving north for lengthy sections while returning home from various vacations in the south. In 1994, Kevin and I would hit the road yet again, enlisting another friend, Tim, as our third party. This trip was far more practical, starting in Akron where we lived instead of driving to Cleveland. We were faithful to 21 south of there, however, reaching Beckley, WV. the first night. The next day we set a goal of Columbia, SC, which we would ultimately make; however, we had to cheat a bit and skip the rather desolate sec-

tion of 21 in northern South Carolina in lieu of I-77 for time's sake. On the third day we reached Hunting Island by mid-day, and having reached our goal, continued on to Savannah, GA. for the remainder of the week.

Three years later, I got the itch again, and took a day in the summer of 1997 to drive, this time alone, to Cleveland, where I would repeat the entire first day of the original 21 trip. Upon reaching Charleston, WV. around 4 pm, I returned home via I-77. I have taken short stretches of 21 since that time, most recently in 2003, and it has been interesting to see various changes in the road, as a lot of the old vestiges of its time as a national highway continue to disappear. While some of the small mom and pop motels and restaurants along the road remain open, most have closed and been replaced by chain motels and restaurants, thus removing a lot of the local color from the roads. The saddest change was when the 1947-era Big Walker Lookout gift shop in Virginia burned to the ground in 2002. This had been one of the most typical 1950s-style tourist attractions along the entire road until that time.

Well, I guess that's progress. At least we have postcards and photos, which are presented in the following pages, and hopefully they can give the reader a sense of what Old 21 was like, whether it was being traveled by West Virginians going north to work, or any northerners traveling south on vacation, or anyone nowadays who prefers the rustic scenery and has the time to take the old road. That's definitely me...

U.S. Route 21 in Ohio

As mentioned previously, U.S. 21 officially appeared in 1926 when the national highway system was first established. In Ohio, however, all of the sections of 21 had previously existed as numbered state highways. Some of these roads had been in use for nearly a century as early stagecoach lines between cities. A 1915 state map shows the roads existing but having no numbered routes, making it challenging to travel from city to city. The same map includes driving directions from Cleveland to Akron along what would later become Route 21 (shown below), utilizing existing landmarks; clearly a more organized system of routes was needed for a public that would become increasingly mobile in the coming years as automobiles became more commonplace. At that time, the road was paved in cities, but in rural areas it was graded and left unpaved. Interestingly, while most of this route follows 21, the first 3.8 miles out of Public Square follow a different route, using Euclid Avenue, Ninth Street, Woodland Avenue, and E. 55th Street to get to Broadway. Why a different route was chosen for the U.S. highway a decade later is unknown.

Within a few years, a system of numbered state routes had developed, simplifying travel throughout the region. Looking at what would later become Route 21, the road began at Public Square in downtown Cleveland as state Route 13, and continued south along the exact path of 21 to New Philadelphia. At that point, Route 13 continued southeast, ending in Bridgeport on the Ohio River. In New Philadelphia, however, state Route 20 continued south along what would become 21, much of it still unpaved, to Newcomerstown. It then continued east toward Columbus, but state Route 8 followed what would become 21 the remainder of the way to Marietta on the Ohio River. Like 21, Route 8's northern end was at Public Square, but the latter took a different course south, through Akron and Canton. The two roads met briefly in New Philadelphia but took different paths to Newcomerstown.

	CLEVELAND TO AKRON (via Brecksville)—34.9 Miles.
0.0	Leave Public Square at Monument corner and go east on Euclid Ave. with trolleys to first four-corners.
0.3	Turn to right (southeast) with trolleys onto Ninth St. Asphalt pavement.
0.5	Erie Street Cemetery on left.
0.8	End of Ninth St. Turn to left onto Woodland Ave. with trolleys.
1.2	Catholic church on left.
2.0	Case-Woodland School on right.
2.4	At five-corners. Turn square to right (south) with trolleys onto Ffty-fifth St. Granite cobblestone pavement 2.3 miles.
2.8	Cross long bridge.
3.5	Under railroad viaduct.
3.8	Bear to left (southeast) with trolleys onto Broadway.
4.2	Cross railroad.
4.4	Bend right.
4.7	Fire Department house at left. Turn right (south) onto Seventy-first St., leaving trolleys. Brick pavement 12.7 miles.
5.2	Pick up and follow trolleys and leave same at 5.4 miles.
5.7	Under railroad viaduct.
6.0	Narrow pavement.
6.2	Cross two railroad viaducts.
7.2	Go slow down long hill, making wide bend to left (east).
7.5	Cross railroad and turn to right (south) across large iron bridge over canal and Cuyahoga River.
7.9	WILLOW. Depot on left. Cross railroad and bend left.
8.0	Up winding hill 0.4 mile long.
9.3	Cemetery on left.
9.8	Up long hill.
10.1	INDEPENDENCE. Postoffice on right.
10.3	School on left.
12.8	Slow. Bend left.
13.3	Slow. Bend right.
14.3	Down hill across iron bridge, then up hill.
14.6	BRECKSVILLE.
16.4	School on left.
17.5	End of pavement. Cross county line between Cuyahoga and Summit Counties. Clay road with some gravel for 11.2 miles.
18.6	Slow. Bend right and go down hill 0.4 mile long.
19.0	Cross bridge at foot of hill.
19.3	Cross bridge and up short hill.
20.0	Slow. Bend left. Small cemetery on right.
20.2	RICHFIELD. Crossroad. Straight ahead.
22.1	School on right.
23.8	HAMMONDS CORNERS or BATH.
24.3	Slow. Down hill and bend right.
24.9	Slow. Up over hill.
25.1	BATH CENTER.
25.3	Slow. Bend left, then right.
25.6	Cross bridge, then bend right, then left.
25.9	GHENT. Cross iron bridge, then keep to right and go up steep hill. (Road leading to left at foot of hill is now being macadamized and when finished will be the better route.)
26.1	Bend left at top of hill.
27.5	MONTROSE. Turn to left (east) at crossroad.

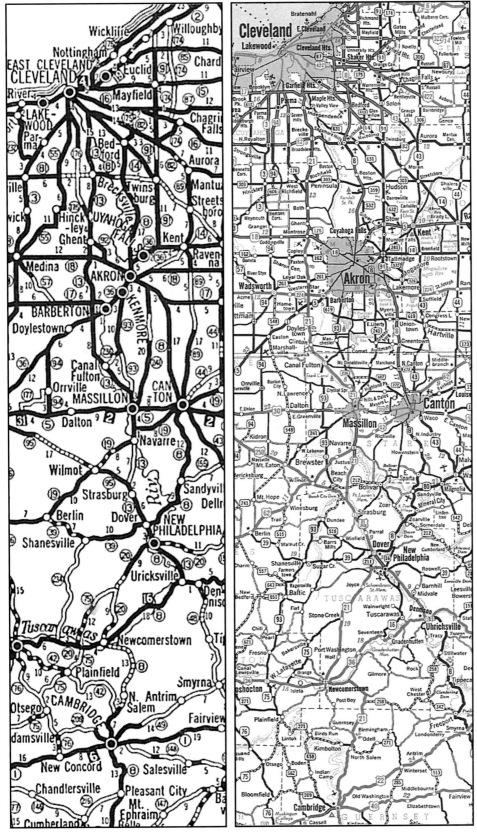

(far left) 1925 Ohio map, showing the original state route system [state route numbers are in circles], just one year before the U.S. Highway system was put into use. Many of these intial state highways are still in place today. This can be contrasted to the 1948 map at near left, showing the course of U.S. 21 in somewhat better detail.

After the inception of the national highway system in 1926, many routes were renumbered or in some cases realigned entirely. Route 8 continued to exist, but its southern section was rerouted further east, ending at the Ohio River in the village of Fly. In later years, 8 was broken into two segments, both of which exist today. One travels just from Cleveland to Akron, and the other, renamed as Route 800, travels from Canton to Fly. Meanwhile, state Route 20 ceased to exist, the number being taken by U.S. Route 20, and the state Route 13 designation was reused for a road running north and south through Central Ohio.

Traveling on 21 through Ohio is complicated by the fact that it lost its national highway designation in 1971, and even before that, various sections were realigned onto bypasses and highways over the years, so that maps from different periods would show 21 on different roads. The following is a general description of the road over its five-state course, both in its original

13

alignment as well as with its various reroutings over the years, for any adventurous souls who are looking for an interesting and scenic drive through cities, farmlands, the hills and mountains of Appalachia, and the rural South.

The official starting point for Route 21 (mile 0) was at the center of Cleveland's Public Square, at the intersection of Ontario Street and Superior Avenue. Superior also carries U.S. Routes 6 (the nation's second-longest highway, traveling more than 3,200 miles from Provincetown, MA. to Bishop, CA., although it originally traveled all the way to Long Beach) and 20 (the nation's longest highway, traveling more than 3,300 miles from Boston, MA. to Newport, OR.), and this central point is also the western end of U.S.

(above) The official starting point for Route 21, at the center of Cleveland's Public Square, as it appeared in the late 1960s. The Soldiers and Sailors Monument is in the background; the two buildings on the left were imploded in 1982 to make way for what is now the 45-story BP building. At the extreme lower right is a 21 sign, with a one-way arrow pointing south; (below) Another view of Route 21's origin, looking south.

Route 322 (which travels east through northern Pennsylvania, ending in Atlantic City, N.J.), as well as being the northern end of U.S. Route 42 (which travels southwest from here to Louisville, KY.). 21's

path took it south on Ontario Street out of the square, and in so doing, it shared the road with U.S. Route 422 (traveling from this point east to the outskirts of Philadelphia, PA.), as well as Ohio state routes 8 (traveling south to the Ohio River), 14 (traveling southeast to the Pennsylvania state line), 43 (traveling southeast to the Ohio River at Steubenville), and 87 (traveling east to the town of Kinsman). On the way out of the square, the city's Terminal Tower complex (completed in 1930) stands to the right, with the Soldiers and Sailors Monument (completed in 1894) on the left. Cleveland is by far the largest city along the course of 21, with a most recent population estimate of 433,000, although that is down from a peak of more than 900,000 residents in 1950, when it was the nation's sixth-largest city. Cuyahoga County still has an overall population of nearly 1.4 million.

Soon after leaving the square, the first major landmark on the left is the home of the Cleveland Cavaliers basketball

(above left) The Terminal Tower remains one of Cleveland's most visible symbols after eighty years; (left) Looking north along Ontario Street (Old 21) toward Tower City, the area surrounding the tower.

(left) Quicken Loans Arena, formerly known as Gund Arena, is home to the NBA Cleveland Cavaliers, and it stands in the foreground along Ontario Avenue, with city's three tallest buildings (Terminal Tower, Key Tower, and BP Building) in the background; (below left) Immediately south of the arena is Progressive Field, formerly known as Jacobs Field, home to the Cleveland Indians baseball team.

team, Quicken Loans Arena (formerly known as Gund Arena). Immediately south of that is the home of the Cleveland Indians baseball team, Progressive Field (formerly known as Jacobs Field), standing at the intersection of Ontario and Carnegie Avenue. After crossing Carnegie Avenue, the road crosses under Interstate 90 (the nation's longest interstate, traveling 3,100 miles from Boston to Seattle, WA.), very close to the northern end of Interstate 77, the road that ultimately replaced 21 in Ohio. After crossing under I-90, the route turns right at the next major intersection onto Broadway, which then continues southeast away from downtown, running parallel to a major line of railroad tracks. South of the inter-section of Rockefeller Avenue, the road was originally known as Broadway Extension, and later as Pittsburgh Avenue, before eventual-ly being renamed as Broadway. 21 continued on this road to its inter-section with E. 34th, at which point it turned right and continued as Broadway. The original alignment of 21 had it turn right at Rockefeller Avenue (which was the original Broadway), continuing through a bleakly industrial section of the city

N. Easterly Along N. Side Broadway From E. 9th St.

(right) Two photos of Broadway on the city's near east side in 1927; new shield-shaped 21 signs are seen in both photos, along with Ohio-shaped state Route 8 signs. In the bottom photo, the Terminal Tower can be seen at far left, under con-struction. None of the buildings seen here along Broadway are standing today [from the Cleveland Union Terminal Collection, a remarkably massive array of photos of this huge urban project, taken in the late 1920s, courtesy of the Cleveland State University Library collection].

Westerly Along N. Side Broadway From E. 15th St.

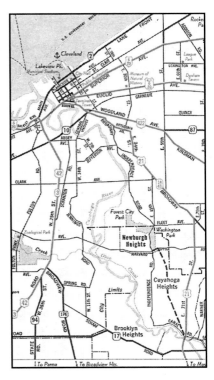

before reconnecting with modern-day Broadway at E. 34th Street. Needless to say, this is one of the most confusing sections of 21 to retrace in all of Ohio, although a good city map can shed some light on the route's alignment.

Skirting the city's industrial Flats district, Broadway soon passes to the north of the prominent Blast Furnace of ArcelorMittal Steel, for-

(left) Cleveland map from 1948, showing the second alignment of 21 on Pittsburgh Avenue and East 34th Street, before both roads were renamed as Broadway and old Broadway was renamed as Rockefeller; (above) Blast Furnace of ArcelorMittal Steel, formerly Republic and then LTV Steel, at Broadway and E. 45th.

merly Republic and then LTV Steel, at E. 45th St. This landmark is known to many Clevelanders by the flames that frequently burned from the plant's two large smokestacks at night, making a spectacle visible from long distances. Just past the factory, Broadway crosses over I-77 for the first of many times along 21's entire course. 21 then continued along Broadway until reaching E. 71st Street, where it turned right to head south out of the Cleveland area.

Heading south on E. 71st St., the road briefly passes through the village of Cuyahoga Heights, with its population of 599. At the south end of the village, the road travels down a long slope toward the Cuyahoga Valley, where lies another challenge for those tracing old 21, as there is a confluence of Old 21, the Willow Freeway, Cuyahoga River, Ohio and Erie Canal, two railroad lines, and state Route 17 (a route limited to southern Cuyahoga County, traveling from North Olmsted to Bedford Heights). This is an area known historically as Willow, and although it was never a town as such, it seems to have existed primarily as a railroad stop, as there was a Willow station along the B& O Railroad at that point. Originally 21 continued past the station, crossing the river and canal before climbing the hill on the far side of the valley, along what is now Old Brecksville Road. In October 1940, however, a cloverleaf intersection was opened just south of the river crossing, allowing for better traffic flow at the crossing of 21 and Route 17. One of the first such cloverleafs in the state, it defined the area in some ways, with several businesses in the area using the word cloverleaf in their names even to this day. A second, far larger cloverleaf was

(left) Northern end of state Route 21, at the entrance to I-77 at E. 71st St.; (right) Aerial view of the 1940 cloverleaf at the intersection of Brecksville Rd. (the vertical road) and state Route 17 (horizontal road), at the northern boundary of Independence.

built nearby years later, at the intersection of I-77 and I-480.

Following Old 21 south in this area is difficult because of the rerouting of the road over the years. With the original road no longer existing, one comes to the end of E. 71st St. at the bottom of the hill, and must turn left on Canal Road, followed by a right on Warner Road, another right on Granger Road, and then a right onto the southbound ramp of the cloverleaf, putting one back on 21, which is known from this point south as Brecksville Road. Tracing the road north is considerably easier, as one continues on Brecksville Rd. until it becomes an entrance ramp for I-77, just past the cloverleaf. Just before entering the freeway, there is an exit to the right, which puts one onto E. 71st St. to continue north.

I-77 from this point north into the city is one of the state's oldest sections of highway, known originally as the Willow Freeway, to which it is sometimes referred even today. This four-lane highway had originally been proposed in 1927 as a route to connect with a proposed east-west highway through downtown Cleveland. The cloverleaf was the first section completed, at a cost of nearly $1.2 million (some of which was funded by the WPA), although construction of the remainder of the highway was delayed for five years by World War II. When it was finally completed, the highway bypassed all of E. 71st St., ending at E. 49th St. near Broadway, after which 21 was rerouted onto the highway. In 1962, construction began on the northernmost section of the freeway, which would take it to the Innerbelt (today Interstate 90) just south of downtown. This portion was completed in 1966, although 21 was not routed onto that last segment, instead continuing to follow Broadway into town. All of the Willow Freeway was later incorporated into I-77 and remains in service today.

South of the Willow area, Brecksville Rd. is numbered as state Route 21, continuing along the U.S. route's final alignment before being eliminated in 1971. Sixty miles in length, state Route 21 consists partly of limited access highway and partly of two- or four-lane suburban and country roads, and ends just north of Strasburg in Tuscarawas County. While some maps show state Route 21 continuing into downtown Cleveland along I-77, this is incorrect as its northern endpoint is at its junction with 77 in Cuyahoga Heights.

From Willow south to just beyond the Summit County line, 21 was upgraded to four lanes in 1946. After leaving Willow, the road travels through the city of Independence, population 7,100. It soon crosses over Interstate 480, one of the city's major suburban outer belts, before passing the city's public square (mile 10), where several Victorian-era public buildings can be seen. Brecksville Rd. then continues south into the city of Brecksville, with a population just over 13,000. Founded in 1811 during the early development of the Western Reserve, the city is known largely for the extensive sections of

(above) Century-old firehouse, now in use as the local historical society, near the public square of Independence; (right) The Spanish Tavern restaurant along 21 in Brecksville, as seen in the 1970s; it remains in business today with new management as Hunters Pub.

(above) View of Brecksville Road around 1900, looking north from the intersection with Route 82; (above right) Ye Old Stage Coach Inn was a restaurant set in this old stagecoach stop, built in 1839. This gives one an idea of the age of Brecksville Road in this area. An unusual U.S. 21 sign stands in front of the building, with a white background and a shield outline. The building remains standing today, but has been converted to office space; (right) Inside the restaurant in the 1950s.

the Cleveland Metropark system and Cuyahoga Valley National Park that lie within its boundaries. At the city's central point (mile 15), 21 crosses state Route 82 (traveling east and west from Elyria to Masury in Trumbull County) and continues south through a typical suburban setting, with a change toward light industry further south.

At mile 17, Route 21 leaves Cuyahoga County and crosses into Summit County and the Village of Richfield, with a population of nearly 3,300, after which it soon passes the Ohio Turnpike entrance. Built in the early 1950s, the turnpike carries the designation of Interstate 80, and it connects with the Pennsylvania Turnpike on the east end and the Indiana Turnpike on the west end. This provides a direct route from both New York City and Philadelphia westward to Chicago and eventually the West Coast. Originally, once crossing the county line, 21 became known as Cleveland-Massillon Road. However, the road now retains its Brecksville Road name throughout Richfield Township.

Both north and south of the turnpike, several small motels appeared after that road's opening. Two of these are shown here, although only the Rainbow/Quality Courts motel re-

(left) Ohio Turnpike entrance in Richfield Township; (above) A huge Veterans Administration hospital stands on the west side of 21, on the south end of Brecksville.

mains standing today, operating as a Motel 6. Immediately south of the turnpike was the Brushwood Inn, built in 1960, but which was razed during turnpike renovations in the early 2000s. In place of these smaller motels are several modern chain motels such as Hampton Inn, Holiday Inn Express, etc. A few of the area's 1950s-era businesses remain today, such as the Richfield Family Restaurant, a Dairy Queen, a miniature golf course, etc. This area represents the southernmost extent of "Greater Cleveland" along Route 21; south of this, the road takes on a distinctly more rural appearance.

Shortly after passing the turnpike, state Route 21 follows a southbound ramp to join I-77, bypassing the old road all the way to southern Stark County. For those going north on the old road, however, there is no entrance ramp to 77/21 going either north or south, so travelers on that road need to go past the freeway and turn around to enter it, or travel two miles further north to Miller Road, where 77 can be accessed easily. State Route 21 continues into Copley Township ten miles south, where 77 splits and goes eastward toward Akron, while "New 21", or Great Lakes Boulevard, as it is officially named, continues south. This four-lane road bypasses Copley, Barberton, Canal Fulton, and Massillon, joining "Old 21" just north of Navarre. Built over several years, this upgraded portion of 21 opened in 1964.

Returning to the old road in Richfield, it continues south after crossing under I-77, soon passing an old white house, known as Farnham Manor. Built in 1834 by some of the area's earliest settlers, the home (which is currently vacant) gives an idea of the road's age, as this section appeared some time between the earliest settling of the area, circa 1809, and the construction of the house. Further south is Whitey's restaurant, a staple of Northeast Ohio dining since 1953; it remains extremely popular to this day, largely for its hamburger menu. Soon after this comes the intersection

(left) Nineteenth-Century stagecoach stop at Old 21 and 303, now renovated to house small businesses.

19

(left) The Ohio Motel, in northern Bath Township, remains in business today; (below) Poor Richard's Pub (now known as Ken Stewart's Lodge) and Lanning's Restaurant, both on 21 in Bath, are two of the area's finest restaurants; (bottom right) St. Luke's century-old church building in Ghent has been converted into an exercise and health spa in recent years.

with state Route 303 in Richfield Center (mile 21). Originally, this was the main intersection in the township, with West Richfield one mile west at the intersection of Routes 303 and 176. In more recent years, the latter intersection has become the central commercial area of Richfield. An old inn from the stagecoach days remains at the northwest corner of 303 and Brecksville Rd, now housing small businesses.

Continuing south, Old 21 passes the site of the Skyline Theater, one of the area's many outdoor drive-in movie theaters of the 1950s and 60s. Named for the view of the Cuyahoga Valley from this point looking east, the theater had closed by the 1980s, and one small building from the complex is all that remains today. Just past this is the intersection with Interstate 271, which goes from the Cleveland area southwest to Interstate 71, which then continues to Columbus and Cincinnati. After that is the intersection with state Route 176, which travels northward, parallel to 21, ending on Cleveland's southwest side. 176 was one of the original state routes laid out in the 1920s, and originally traveled from downtown Akron west, joining 21 in Ghent and sharing the road for several miles before veering west at this point. In later years the road was truncated here, with its southern portions losing their route designation.

Continuing south, the road passes an area known as Terry Point, one of the highest spots in Summit County. South of this is an area with numerous terminals for several major trucking companies, although in recent years many of these have closed and stand empty. This was at one time a major center for transportation due to its proximity with I-77, 271, and the turnpike, but due to the economic downturn in the 2000s, the area is no longer thriving as it once did. The road then crosses into Bath Township, a pleasant area of rolling hills and wealthy homeowners with a population of nearly 10,000, founded in 1818. From here south to the county line, Old 21 is known as Cleveland-Massillon Road. Hammond's Corners, at the intersection with Ira Road, is the first commercial area encountered, followed two miles later by Bath Center (mile 26), site of the town hall.

Descending gradually into the valley of Yellow Creek, 21 soon enters the village of Ghent. While unincor-

porated, Ghent (in conjunction with the Montrose district two miles south) is considered a "census-designated place" for statistical purposes. Ghent's origins are in the early 1800s like the rest of the township, when several mills were established along Yellow Creek. Upon entering Ghent, 21 bears to the left, with a small side road continuing straight. Known as Wye Road, this side road crosses the creek and then travels up a steep and winding grade out of the village, connecting with 21 further south. This road was part of the original stagecoach run from Cleveland south, although in the 1915 map shown earlier, it can be seen that what is now Cleveland-Massillon Road going southeast out of the village and up a more gradual grade, was just being paved. By the time of U.S. 21's formation a decade later, this was the main road through the area, so that Wye Road was never part of 21 itself. Following Old 21 to the top of the hill, it then bears right at the intersec-

tion with Ghent Road (although signs point one to the left to join up with state 21 and I-77, the entrance to which is around the curve). Just past this on the left stood Jimbo's drive-in, a typical 1950s-style restaurant, which operated from 1959 until the early 1990s. It has stood empty now for more than a decade.

Crossing over 77 again just a half-mile south of this, Old 21 soon enters the Montrose district mentioned earlier. The center of this is the intersection with state Route 18 (mile 28), the main road going east into Akron and west to the Indiana state line.

Montrose is another unincorporated area, consisting of portions of the City of Fairlawn, Bath, and Copley Townships. Until the 1970s, it consisted of little more than a few small businesses, but in recent years it has seen extensive commercial growth and is now one of the county's most con-

gested areas. After passing through Montrose, 21 enters Copley Township, with its population of over 13,000. The road soon passes under 77 yet again while continuing straight south, eventually reaching Copley Circle, at the intersection with state Route 162 (mile 31), which travels from Akron to Republic in western Ohio. A small gazebo stands in the circle, with several century-old buildings nearby.

Continuing south, the commercialism soon disappears in favor of rolling hills and countryside. Approximately one mile south of the circle, Foster's Motel was a small motor court that operated on the east side of the road until the 1970s, although there are no remains of it today. Beyond this, the road crosses Wolf Creek, which is dammed to

form the Barberton Reservoir. The road then ascends a hill via a narrow cut through solid rock; at the top of the hill on the left is the Wolf Creek Winery, with its view of the reservoir. Beyond this is the unincorporated village of Loyal Oak, at the

(above left) Gazebo in the center of Copley Circle; (above) Barberton Reservoir, formed from Wolf Creek, in southern Copley Township; (left) Loyal Oak Tavern, built as a hotel in 1840 and operating as a tavern/restaurant since 1875.

(right) Loyal Oak Country Store building, built in 1828; (below) Loyal Oak cider mill, built in 1874

intersection with state Route 261, which travels from Kent to Wadsworth. At the southeast corner of this intersection is the Loyal Oak Tavern, built as a hotel around 1840. At the opposite corner is a building originally housing the local country store, built in 1828 as a stagecoach stop along the road from Cleveland to the Ohio River. On the community's north side is a wooden apple cider mill, built in 1874 as a sawmill, and converted to a cider mill five years later by owner John J. Knecht. It is still owned by his descendants today, and it remains in operation during special events. After leaving Loyal Oak, 21 continues

south, crossing I-76/modern U.S. 224, which travels from Camden, N.J. to Westfield Center, OH. (where it connects to I-71).

At mile 36, the road comes to the center of the city of Norton, with a population of more than 11,000. The center is at Norton Avenue, which is "Old" U.S. Route 224, traveling from New Castle, PA. to Huntington, IN. The road then passes through the western portion of the city of Barberton, population nearly 28,000, at which point it is known as 31st Street NW. Upon crossing Wooster Road (formerly state Route 5 but no longer designated as such) at a locality known as Johnson's Corners, the road becomes 31st Street SW. Soon after this intersection, the road curves to the left, becoming Cleveland-Massillon Road again, while 31st St. bears straight into a residential area. The road then continues through an increasingly rural setting for several miles before reaching the Village of Clinton (mile 43), the first of several Ohio & Erie Canal towns through which the road passes.

Clinton, with a population just over 1,300, was established in 1816 and grew quickly when the canal was opened in this area in 1828, and eventually it merged with the village of Warwick on the west side of the canal. The canal peaked in operation during the mid-1800s, but by the 1870s its business had largely been taken over by the railroads. In 1913 a catastrophic flood destroyed much of what was left of the canal, although many of the actual waterways remain in place to this day. The canal runs parallel to the Tuscarawas River, and Old 21 was built parallel to the canal from Clinton south to Navarre. In recent years, the towpath along the canal has been renovated as part of the 110-mile Ohio & Erie Canal Heritage Canalway, from Cleveland to Dover in Tuscarawas County.

(right) Built in the 1870s, the three-story Limbach Block on Main Street was the first brick building in Clinton. The Limbach Brothers, who built the Italianate structure, incorporated an abandoned canal boat into its foundation as a way to prevent it from settling into the area's swampy ground. The building remains standing today.

(left) Horses pulling a canal boat at Canal Fulton; (below) Massillon Brewing Co. plant, circa 1880s; today Old 21 travels directly through this site.

Upon arriving in Clinton, Route 21 took a left onto Main Street, crossing the river, canal, and railroad tracks and then proceeding through the middle of the village. After several blocks, 21 then turned right, with this southern section again named as Cleveland-Massillon Road. Another mile south, the road crosses into Stark County, at which point it is renamed as Erie Avenue NW, still paralleling the canal immediately to the west. Two miles from the county line, the road enters the city of Canal Fulton (mile 46), population 5,000; here the road is briefly renamed as High Street NE. Upon reaching the intersection of Cherry Street (state Route 93, which travels from Akron to Ironton on the Ohio River), 21 turns right, going two blocks on Cherry before taking a left onto South Canal Street. Near this intersection is the Canalway Center, where visitors can take a ride on the St. Helena III, an authentic reproduction of a canal boat, towed by horses along the canal. Once on S. Canal St., 21 travels south out of town, at which time its name reverts to Erie Avenue NW.

Five miles further south, the road travels through the locality of Crystal Springs, formerly known at Millport, at the intersection of state Route 236 (which travels from southern Summit County to Massillon). 21 travels through the site of the Massillon Brewing Company plant, built in 1876 as a flour mill. Facing the canal, the plant brewed beer that was carried in specially designed canal boats to Massillon for bottling and distribution. It burned to the ground in 1913, leaving no remains today.

Soon after this, the road enters the outskirts of the city of Massillon (population just over 31,000), at which point the road is renamed as 1st Street NE. At this point, New 21 is visible just one block to the west; that road was built over the site of the canal through Massillon. At mile 55, the road reaches the center of town at the intersection with Lincoln Way, which was the original alignment of the Lincoln Highway, or U.S. Route 30, through the city. Opened in 1913, the Lincoln Highway was the

(above left) Downtown Massillon, looking east along the Lincoln Highway around 1960; a U.S. 21 and turnpike sign are visible in the lower right section; (left) Lincoln Way in downtown Massillon at night, looking west, in the 1940s.

23

(right) Some of the buildings in the Massillon State Hospital, early Twentieth Century

country's first coast-to-coast road, stretching from New York City to San Francisco. Later, Route 30 was routed differently, stretching more than 3,000 miles from Atlantic City, NJ. to Astoria, OR. In later years, the local portion was rerouted onto a modern highway running south of Canton and Massillon. Upon reaching Lincoln Way, Old 21 turns west for two blocks before turning left on Erie Street S, now numbered as state Route 241, which travels from Akron to Millersburg.

Going approximately two miles south on Erie Street S, the road gradually leaves downtown before curving to the west to join the New 21 highway at its southern end. Just at the curve, the original alignment of 21 briefly continues south as Nave Road SE, which travels into the Massillon State Hospital complex. Opened in 1898 as the Massillon State Hospital for the Insane, the complex consisted of numerous buildings of grand Victorian style, and by 1950 it housed over 3,000 residents. Today the complex consists of several smaller buildings and is known as the Massillon Psychiatric Center. A large, abandoned, century-old building in the complex was destroyed by fire in 2008.

Meanwhile, Erie Street curves to meet New 21, just north of the intersection with the modern highway that carries U.S. Routes 30 and 62. South of this, state Route 21 continues as Erie Street S, now a two-lane road. For the next four miles, 21 runs in conjunction with U.S. 62, one of the lengthier U.S. highways, traveling from Niagara Falls at the Canadian border to El Paso, TX. at the Mexican border. Soon the road travels into the village of Navarre, with its population of just over 1,400, at which point the road is known as Main Street. Named after a region in Spain, this is the last canal town encountered along this stretch of 21. In the downtown area (mile 61), the smell of fresh bread is usually in the air as the road passes the headquarters for Nickles Bakery, a prominent regional chain. Just south of this, U.S. 62 turns to the southwest along Canal Street, with 21 continuing south across the Tuscarawas River and Ohio & Erie Canal again.

After leaving Navarre, the road travels through a lengthy rural stretch before descending a hill from which the Beach City airport is visible to the west. At the bottom of the hill, the road crosses state Route 212, which travels from nearby Beach City east into rural Harrison County. This intersection is at the Tuscarawas County line, and just one mile south of this, Ohio Route 21 ends at the intersection with U.S. Route 250, a road which travels from Sandusky, OH. to Richmond, VA. Old 21, however, continued south in conjunction with 250 for several miles into New Philadelphia. Soon after the

The Junction Restaurant/gas station, seen in the late 1950s, stood at the intersection of Routes 21 and 250, just north of Strasburg [courtesy of Fred Miller, Tuscarawas County Historical Society].

WOOSTER AVENUE, LOOKING SOUTH
STRASBURG, O.

The Garver Bros. Co., World's Largest Country Store, Strasburg, O.

(left) Postcard showing a scene along Wooster Avenue in Strasburg in the 1940s, outside of a Canfield Gas station; this appears to be the best known photograph of an original embossed U.S. 21 shield sign, along with a U.S. 250 sign [courtesy of Fred Miller at the Tuscarawas County Historical Society]; (below left) Garver Brothers store in Strasburg, circa 1940s.

junction with 250 comes the outskirts of the village of Strasburg (mile 70), with its population of 2,300. Known as North and South Wooster Avenue through this area, 21/250 passes the former site of a large brick building housing the Garver Store Flea Market. This was originally Garver Bros. department store, which operated from 1866 to 1970 and was well-known through the area. The building was destroyed by fire in October 2010.

Once beyond Strasburg, the road crosses Sugar Creek just as it reaches I-77 yet again. At this point, U.S. 250 enters the highway to bypass Dover and New Philadelphia, before turning east six miles to the south. This section of the interstate was completed in 1967, at which time 21 and 250 were both rerouted onto it. Prior to that, however, original Routes 21 and 250 continued straight on South Wooster Avenue (now County Highway 74), briefly being known as Columbia Road as it passes through the unincorporated and unmarked village of Columbia. Immediately after this is another unmarked locality known as Loudon. This quickly leads into the Village of Parral, with a population of 241, at which point the road again goes by the name of Wooster Avenue.

Wooster Avenue then continues into the City of Dover, with a population of just over 12,000. Laid out in 1806 and at one time known as Canal Dover, the town is bisected by the Tuscarawas River and the Ohio & Erie Canal, which Wooster Avenue crosses just after joining state Route 800 (mile 76). 800 is the southern portion of what was formerly state Route 8, which begins at Cleveland's Public Square just like 21, and ends now in Akron. 800 then begins on the south side of Canton and follows old Route 8 to the Ohio River at the tiny village of Fly. As noted at the beginning of this chapter, prior to 1926, what later became U.S. Route 21 south of Newcomerstown was the original alignment of Route 8. Upon crossing the river, the road passes an unremarkable two-story yellow brick building standing just to

(right) Two views of Biederman's Amoco gas station on the east side of 21 in Parral, circa 1940s; note the price of gas: 26 9/10 cents [courtesy of Fred Miller, Tuscarawas County Historical Society].

the west; this was originally the Tuscarawas Valley Brewing Co. plant, where beer was brewed between 1906 and 1914. The upper floors were later dynamited away and the remaining portion is used today as a machine shop. Three blocks past this, Wooster Avenue ends, with Old 21 and 800 turning left onto East Iron Blvd.

East Iron Blvd. travels east for several blocks before turning south and being renamed as Boulevard Street. At this point the road passes Dover Union Hospital, founded in 1903. Soon after this, it enters the city of New Philadelphia, the county seat, with a population of just over 17,000. Here it is known as 4th Street NW and it continues approximately one mile south before 800 turns east on Ray Avenue. Old 21 continued south, bypassing downtown and the city's ornate county courthouse (why 21 was never routed through the city's downtown area is unclear), until reaching West High Street, where it turned right to travel west out of the city. This section of West High is numbered as state Route 39, which travels from Crawford County in north central Ohio to East Liverpool near the Ohio River. It is also numbered as Business Route 250, between I-77/250 and downtown. 21 goes out of the town along this road, through a commercial district, before crossing under 77 again at

Exit 81. From the mid-1950s through 1967, however, 21 was rerouted to the west beginning in Dover, where it traveled from Wooster Avenue two blocks west on Third Street before continuing south on South Tuscarawas Avenue. It then crossed the river and continued two miles into New Philadelphia, where it reached High Street, turning right (west) and leaving the city [thanks to Fred Miller of the Tuscarawas County Historical Society for tracking that down].

Immediately after crossing 77, the road turns south, now numbered as County Road 21. This is roughly the half-way point (mile 82) from Cleveland to the Ohio River, and the vast majority of the remaining road in Ohio travels through very rural territory. The region technically labeled as Appalachia begins in Tuscarawas County and continues south to the Ohio River. From this point south along 21, the countryside is increasingly consistent with this label, with larger and more irregular hills, more curves in the road, and

(left) Dover Union Hospital as it appeared in the 1960s; (below) The Green Gables gas station, seen in the 1940s, stood at the intersection of 21 and state Route 39, west of New Philadelphia; this site is now occupied by a southbound exit lane from I-77; the sign pointing to Dover was routing drivers along Route 39 to bypass New Philadelphia. One can barely see the tiny image of a Route 21 shield at the far left [courtesy of Fred Miller, Tuscarawas County Historical Society, and originally donated by Anne Debevec].

more irregular living conditions, ranging from small run-down buildings and trailer homes to large well-kept structures, often next door to each other with no consistent pattern. Farming and coal mining have traditionally been the largest sources of employment in the region, although most of the coal mining in Ohio was on a relatively small scale and the mines along the course of 21 closed many years ago. As the road travels further into the country, the people become increasingly consistent with the label as well. In the 1994 book "Appalachian Values," by Loyal Jones, those values are summed up as follows:

1. Individualism: often the most obvious Appalachian characteristic: look after oneself; enjoy solitude; freedom from external restraints; do things for oneself; not wanting to be beholding to others; make do; strong work ethic; courage; defend oneself or take revenge, rather than relying on "the law."

2. Strong Sense of Extended Family: family-centered, rather than community-centered; Appalachian people settled in kin-groups, not towns; loyalty runs deep; responsibility may extend beyond immediate family; "blood is thicker than water."

3. Love of Place: the term "homeplace" is common; never forget "back home" and go there as often as possible; sometimes stay in places where there is no hope of maintaining decent lives.

4. Neighborliness and Hospitality: help each other out, but suspicious of strangers; spontaneous to invite people for a meal, to spend the night, etc. People are friendly, but not open to strangers. Trust is important. Tend not to ask your advice until they trust you. Relationships are important and deep relationships are developed slowly. This suspicion of outsiders is based on the exploitative past.

5. Traditionalism: a strong love of tradition; skeptical of schemes for "progress"; love of things as they are. Change comes slowly. This is typical of more isolated areas.

6. Personalism: relates well to others, but think in terms of persons rather than degrees or professional reputations; go to great lengths to keep from offending others; getting along is more important than letting one's feelings be known.

7. Modesty and Being Oneself: believe one should not put on airs; be oneself, not a phony; don't pretend to be something you're not or be boastful; don't get above your raising.

8. Sense of Beauty: displayed through music, folksongs, poems, arts, crafts, etc., colorful language metaphors; home and beauty are closely connected.

9. Sense of Humor: seem dour, but laugh at ourselves; do not appreciate being laughed at; humor sustains people in hard times. Humor is often sarcastic.

10. Strong sense of solidarity: stick, together, even if you disagree, express yourself but stand together, especially against outsiders, government, or big organizations. Unfortunately, this can be counterproductive.

11. Strong sense of Patriotism: goes back to Civil War times; flag, land, and relationships are important.

It is these values that drove Akron's rubber companies to recruit workers from Appalachia (as noted in the introduction), both in southern Ohio and in West Virginia, over workers from other areas. In essence the nature of Appalachia defines Route 21, with more than half of the road travelling through that region in Ohio, West Virginia, Virginia, and North Carolina.

Back on the road, County Road 21 is known as Stonecreek Road NW, and it travels through very picturesque countryside, including the unmarked and unincorporated localities of Joyce and Yorktown, before entering the Village of Stone Creek (mile 88), with its population of 184. The village comes and goes quickly, intersecting state Route 751, which begins here and travels west into Coshocton County. 751 ends at an entrance ramp for 77, which runs parallel to and within sight of 21 throughout this stretch of road. Stonecreek Road turns right after leaving

the town, continuing south, still parallel to the interstate. Six miles later (mile 94), the road travels through the unmarked hamlet of Wolf. Originally known as Wolf Station, the community appears on most early Ohio maps, but today consists of a few scattered houses and is not designated with a sign.

Just past Wolf, 21 begins to drift slightly westward and away from 77, as it approaches the Village of Newcomerstown, population 4,000. Once in the village, 21 is known as North College Street, and it soon passes under the highway carrying U.S. Route 36, which travels

Table Rock is a well-known stone formation on a hill overlooking Wolf [courtesy of Fred Miller, Tuscarawas County Historical Society]

from Uhrichsville, OH. westward to the Rocky Mountain National Park in Colorado. Just south of the highway, the road passes the Cy Young Park, a local baseball field named in honor of professional pitcher Denton T. "Cy" Young, who was born locally and died in the town at the age of 88 in 1955. Young played for several teams over his 22-year career, including the Cleveland Spiders and Cleveland Naps, and along the way amassed 511 wins, the most in baseball history, and a record that will likely never be broken. The annual award for the league's best pitcher is named after Young to this day. Another sports legend by the name of Wayne Woodrow "Woody" Hayes grew up in the area, attending high school in Newcomerstown. Hayes was best known as coach of the Ohio State Buckeyes football team from 1951 to 1978, where he won three national titles.

Continuing on College Street into town (mile 98), 21 turns left on East Canal Street, followed by a right several blocks later on Pilling Street, where it joins state Route 258 (21 bypassed the center of town, which is several blocks to the west). Pilling Street then goes south out of town, crossing the Tuscarawas River one final time as the river travels southwest to Coshocton, where it joins the Walhonding River to form the Muskingum River, which then travels south through Zanesville, eventually reaching the Ohio River at Marietta. Continuing as Route 258, the road then turns east and paral-

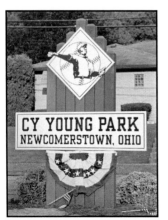

lels the river for several miles until it again passes under I-77. The road eventually turns south away from the river, passing through the unmarked locality of Bernice and onward through very rural territory for seven miles before 258 turns left, continuing onward into Harrison County. 21 then continues south as Salt Fork Road for one mile before crossing into Guernsey County. This section of road, from Newcomerstown to Cambridge and roughly twenty-five miles in length, was the last

(left) Cy Young Park; (right) Part of the memorial to Young

GRANDVIEW CABINS, On U. S. 21, Kimbolton, Ohio
Highly Recommended for the Traveler's Comfort

section of Route 21 in Ohio to be paved with concrete in 1926, completing the route from Cleveland to Marietta, and cutting approximately forty miles off the previously available route. The route was officially numbered with signs after its completion.

Throughout northern Guernsey County, the road is known as Old Twenty One Road, making it easy to follow despite an increasing number of hills and curves in this area. Several miles further south, the road intersects Plainfield Road, which travels west one mile to 77, where it becomes state Route 541, traveling west from this point through the nearby community of Kimbolton and eventually into Knox County. Just south of this is the locality of North Salem (mile 112), and shortly after this, the road passes the Salt Fork State Park, its huge lake, and the earthen dam at its west end. Just past this, the road travels down a hill and under 77 again before moving southwest toward the city of Cambridge.

Cambridge is the Guernsey County seat, with a population of 11,500. Upon entering the city, 21 is renamed as Clark Street, and at the city's northern edge, the road passes Southeastern Ohio Regional Medical Center, the city's only hospital. Clark Street continues south into town, becoming North 11th Street for two blocks before reaching Wheeling Avenue (mile 122), numbered as U.S. Routes 40 and 22. U.S. 40 is one of the country's major east-west routes, beginning in Atlantic City, NJ. and ending in northern Utah (although until 1964 it continued west to San Francisco). It follows the course of the original National Road, built between 1811 and 1839 from Cumberland, MD. to Vandalia, IL., and the Victory Highway, which continued from there to the West Coast. The National Road was one of the country's first improved roads, and to this day, stone mile markers from its early days are a common site along the eastern portions of the road. U.S. 22 travels from Cincinnati through Pittsburgh, eventually ending in Newark, NJ.; its eastern portions are known as the William Penn Highway.

Upon reaching Wheeling Avenue, 21 turns right, going west several blocks until reaching the intersection with state Route 209 (which travels from Byesville to Bloomfield in Muskingum

County), directly in front of the county's court house. At this point the road turns left onto 209, or Southgate Parkway, which passes three times over Wills Creek, a major tributary of the Muskingum River, while continuing south out of the city through a commercial district with numerous motels and restaurants. Route 21's original alignment continued south on 11th Street at Wheeling Avenue, before turning into Morton Avenue, which continued several blocks until 21 turned right onto Woodlawn Avenue, which then travelled another mile before joining in with present-day 209 on the city's south end. This section lost its route designation after the construction of Southgate Parkway. The entire portion of 21 through Cambridge was one of the first in the state to be bypassed, when in 1957 a new stretch of highway was opened one mile east, from Byesville to Cambridge, and this ultimately would become part of I-77. Another segment of highway, stretching from here north to the Kimbolton area, was

(near right) 1925 Ohio map, showing the road from Cambridge to Marietta, which at the time was numbered as state Route 8; (far right) 1948 map of the same area, now renumbered as U.S. 21; (below) Postcard from a Byesville gas station, circa 1950s.

opened in 1964, after which more of 21 was rerouted away from the old road.

Approximately one mile south of the city, 209 crosses Interstate 70, a major east-west highway that has partially replaced U.S. 40 in various areas. It stretches from Baltimore, MD. to central Utah. Soon after this intersection, 209 becomes Southgate Road, and continues approximately four more miles into the Village of Byesville, with its population of nearly 2,600. Upon entering the village, 209 takes a sharp turn to the east, becoming Main Street. Several blocks later, the course of Old 21 turns right onto Depot Street (mile 128), going south out of town. 209 goes straight at this intersection, ending four blocks later at the intersection of I-77. Meanwhile, state Route 821 begins at that same intersection, coming west on Main Street and south on Depot Street. 821 from this point to its termination just north of Marietta follows the exact course of Old 21 through numerous small towns. When the southern portions of 21 were rerouted onto the recently completed 77 in the late 1960s, most of the old road lost its route designation for a few years, although this particular segment, from Byesville to Pleasant City, was designated as state Route 672 for a time (the segment just north of Marietta was numbered as state Route 145). By the early 1970s, however, this entire stretch of Old 21 had been renamed as 821.

After Depot Street/821 leaves the southern village limits, it quickly returns to a rural setting and becomes Marietta Road, letting the traveller know they are on the right path. Four miles beyond Byesville is the unincorporated and unmarked community of Derwent, at the intersection with state Route 313, which travels from Chandlersville in Muskingum County to Batesville in Noble County. Another mile along, the road comes to the village of Pleasant City (mile 133),

population 439. This is at the intersection with state Route 146, which travels from Nashport in Licking County to Summerfield in Noble County. Like most communities along 821, Pleasant City comes and goes quickly as the road continues south. Another half-mile along, 821 crosses into Noble County.

Around this point, the road starts to become noticeably curvier as it extends further into Appalachia. Five miles into the county, 821 passes through the unincorporated community of Ava (mile 139). Consisting of little more than a grouping of homes along a half-mile stretch of road, Ava nevertheless has its own post office and zip code, as well as a monument to the greatest disaster to occur along Route 21: the crash of the U.S.S. Shenandoah airship (see box). Two miles further south is the similarly unincorporated community of Coal Ridge, reminding one of the area's rich mining history. Another two miles goes by before the road enters the village of Belle Valley, with a population of 263. At this point, the road again crosses I-77, which largely cuts the village in half. Although easy to miss, there is a small roadside park two miles south of the village, where there is a memorial to local resident John Gray, who is though to have been the last surviving soldier of the Revolutionary War when he died in 1868 at the age of 104. Across the road from this was the Park Motel, which remains standing although it is no longer in business. Just beyond this is the unincorporated community of Florence. Although it doesn't look like much from the main road, the community actually consists of several blocks's worth of houses, all situated just to the east of the road. Less than half a mile later, the road curves to the east at the local-

The Crash of the U.S.S. Shenandoah

The most famous disaster to occur along Route 21 was the crash of the airship Shenandoah in 1925. Built in Lakehurst, NJ. in 1923,

it was the first of four rigid airships built by the U.S. Navy in the era (the others being the Akron, Macon, and Los Angeles). Officially known as ZR-1, the Shenandoah was built with a metal frame and then filled with huge bags of helium, which was very unusual, as helium was relatively rare at the time. At 680 feet in length and weighing 36 tons, the ship could reach speeds up to 70 mph with engines built by the Packard Motor Company. After its launch in 1923, the Shenandoah became the first rigid airship to cross the North American continent one year later.

In early September 1925, the ship departed on its 57th flight for a lengthy trip in which it was to fly over forty different U.S. cities and various state fairs around the Labor Day holiday. This was primarily a public relations voyage, meant to publicize airship technology to the taxpayers, as well as justify the ship's enormous cost to the same audience. In the early morning of September 3rd, the ship was flying over southern Ohio when it encountered a huge thunderstorm and became caught in an updraft, causing the ship to rise rapidly to 6,000 feet. The violent turbulence put excessive pressure on the ship's metal frame, tearing it into two large sections. The rear section fell to the ground in a field near Ava, killing fourteen crewmen, including the captain, Zachary Lansdowne. The front section was able to remain afloat long enough to gently drift to the ground several miles away, landing along present-day state Route 78, four miles west of Caldwell. Miraculously, all twenty-nine of the crewmen in that section survived.

The remains of the rear section became an immediate tourist attraction, as the photos at left demonstrate. A memorial monument was later built at the site, although due to its remote location, it was later moved to its present position along 821 in the village (shown at bottom, and including a list of those who lost their lives in the disaster). The actual crash site is visible from I-77 just east of Ava; for years a flagpole was the only indication of the crash, although a historical marker was later added. In Ava, a small museum was later established in a trailer along 821, parked outside Rayner's garage and owned and maintained by Bryan and Theresa Rayner.

Two of the three subsequent American rigid airships (Akron and Macon) would also crash, along with the more infamous German airship Hindenberg. By the end of the 1930s, the era of rigid airships was essentially over, although the much smaller (and safer) blimp airships remain a common site to this day.

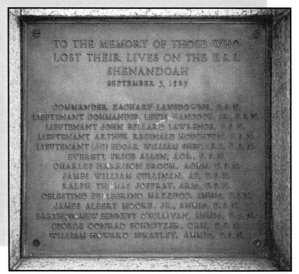

(right) Park Motel, between Belle Valley and Caldwell, in the 1950s; it remains standing today, renamed as the Inn at Belle Valley and surrounded by grown trees, but is no longer in operation; (below right) Local sign on a barn near Caldwell [as seen in 2000] harks back to the very early days along Route 21.

ity of Maple Heights, which consists of another group of scattered houses, just before entering the Village of Caldwell (mile 148).

Caldwell, with a population just shy of 2,000, is the Noble County seat. 821 enters the town as Planing Mill Street, which intersects state Route 285 at its southern end (it travels north to Winterset in Guernsey County); 821 then turns right (south) onto Miller Street, going several blocks before turning left (east) on North Street. Several more blocks pass before the road turns right (south) onto West Street, at the public square. The county courthouse is on the left after the turn, and this central district has a quaint "Main Street USA" look about it. West Street continues south, quickly leading out of town, after which the Marietta Road name returns. One mile south of town, the road crosses state Route 78, which travels from Nelsonville in Athens County all the way to Clarington at the Ohio River. Just east of town along Route 78 is the Thorla-McKee Well, dug in 1814, which was the first oil-producing well in North America. At one time, the area from here south to Macksburg had a number of small oil wells operating, along with coal mines, although oil production in the area had largely ended before 1900. At the Route 78 intersection, I-77 is easily visible less than a half-mile to the west.

Just south of this area is a small subdivision that is marked as South Acres, although it does not appear on any standard maps. Another mile south is the locality of Three Forks, which is unmarked and does not appear on most maps; there appears to be nothing distinguishing this spot in the

Noble County Courthouse in Caldwell

road today. Another mile south of this is the unincorporated locality of Dudley. A sign is there and it appears on older maps, but from the road it appears to consist of little more than a crossroads and a few houses. 821 soon passes under I-77 again, after which it runs on the west side of the interstate for several miles. After another mile, a small side road to the right goes into the unincorporated community of South Olive, which appears to consist of just a few scattered houses. Its unusual name comes from its location in Olive Township; at one time there was also a North Olive, but it has disappeared into history. Immediately past South Olive is the locality of Moundsville, which appears to be little more than a historical relic today. The road then leads directly into Dexter City (mile 155), with its population of 166.

Like Caldwell, Dexter City is located along the West Fork of Duck Creek, a small tributary of the Ohio River along which much of 821 travels. As the road curves south into the town,

(right) Ogle's Dining Room as it appeared in the 1950s; (below left) Monument to Johnny Appleseed, 100 feet south of the restaurant; (below right) Ogle's later restaurant near Macksburg and I-77, three miles south of the original site; it is no longer in business and today houses an adult book store; (bottom left) Castle Hall, an abandoned hotel and Knights of Pythias meeting hall, is one of the most substantial structures remaining in Elba.

it comes within a few hundred feet of I-77 before traveling up a slight grade and past the former

Dexter City school building. Closed in 1964 when it was consolidated with the school in Caldwell, the building more recently held the Dexter City Antique Mall, although that is now closed as well. The road (named as Jefferson Street for this short stretch) then goes through the main part of the village, which actually did resemble the "city" part of its name a century ago, when it contained a hotel, two general stores, the school, a railroad, creamery, post office, restaurant, two doctors, and its own telephone system. Today a cluster of homes, a small store, and the post office are about all that remain (although retaining the latter has been a battle for the village). On the south end of the village is a small yellow brick building that once housed Ogle's Dining Room, operated by Mr. & Mrs. Carl Ogle. Though small, Ogle's was one of the best known landmarks along Old 21 for travelers between West Virginia and northern Ohio. Once the main traffic flow was rerouted onto the interstate in the late 1960s, Ogle's moved to a new location in Macksburg, three miles south at an exit point on the interstate.

Close to the restaurant is a stone marker commemorating John Chapman, better known as Johnny Appleseed, whose brother Parley Chapman was one of the region's earliest settlers, arriving in 1805 after taking a flatboat up Duck Creek to the Dexter City area. John Chapman lived there with his brother for a time while spreading apple seeds around the country.

Continuing another mile south, the road passes the northern end of state Route 339, which

travels south to Porterfield on the Ohio River. Just past this road, 821 enters Washington County, the last of seven counties that 21 crossed through in Ohio. No longer known as Marietta Road, it is now labeled just as State Route 821. Less than a mile from here, the road passes under I-77 again before passing to the west and south of the Village of Macksburg, population 202, at Exit 16 of the interstate. While the original stagecoach line traveled through Macksburg in the 1800s, it appears that Route 21 always bypassed the town before continuing south. Three miles further south is the unincorporated community of Elba, which has a history similar to Dexter City. Once

34

(right) The Elba Community Church stands abandoned in the village; (bottom left) Mail Pouch Tobacco sign painted on a barn along Route 821 just north of Marietta; this is one of the most common scenes in the Appalachian Region; (below right) Wagner's Grocery in Lower Salem, as photographed in 1994, had the look of an earlier era; the sign is no longer there.

home to several hundred residents, Elba also had several coal mines, a hotel, railroad station, several stores, a church, and a post office. By the early 1980s the last store and the post office had closed, and repeated severe flooding along Duck Creek has left just a number of scattered houses, mostly abandoned, along the road today, along with the abandoned Elba Community Church. South of this, the road has an increasing number of hills and curves as it works its way closer to the Ohio River Valley.

Five miles south of Elba is the unincorporated community of Warner, at the intersection of state Route 530, which travels west to Lowell on the Muskingum River. Entering the town as West Street, 821 turns east on Main Street and passes the few blocks of homes before continuing east one mile to the village of Lower Salem (mile 166), with a population of 109. State Route 145 intersects the road here, traveling north into Belmont County. As noted previously, during the brief period in the late 1960s and early 1970s when 21 was routed onto I-77 and the old road no longer had a route designation, the stretch south of here was numbered as a portion of Route 145. This ended when 821 was created shortly thereafter. While in Lower Salem, Main Street turns south to become Whipple Road, which is then renamed as Old Plank Road once outside the village. After another mile, the road passes the locality of Bonn, which appears to be nothing but a historical artifact today. Two miles further, the road passes the unincorporated community of Whipple, which has its own post office and zip code despite consisting of little more than a few scattered homes in the Duck Creek Valley. By this time, the road seems very isolated, typically with minimal traffic and being some distance from the interstate.

Continuing south, the road begins to rise out of the valley, and two miles further along it crosses I-77 again at Exit 6. From here, 821 begins to descend rapidly into the valley of the Muskingum River, and although the road runs closely parallel to 77 over the next mile, the interstate remains at a higher elevation and is quickly out of sight. 821, known as Cambridge Road

through this brief stretch, then winds further down the hill to the locality of Unionville, near the river. This section of the road was significantly widened, with several of its curves straightened, in the early 2000s, so it could be used as an alternate truck route out of Marietta. While Unionville appears to be little more than another historical relic, it is significant as the end point of Route 821, at the junction of state Route 60, which travels south into Marietta and

(left) The Towne Motel along Route 60/Old 21 north of Marietta, as seen in the 1950s; it remains in business today as a Best Western Inn and has doubled in size.

north all the way to Vermilion on Lake Erie.

Old 21 turns left here, going south as Muskingum Drive through the locality of Rathbone on the northern end of Marietta. The Muskingum River runs immediately to the west of the road from here south to the Ohio River. Passing both the Marietta Memorial Hospital and the county fairgrounds, the road then becomes 3rd Street as it enters the main section of Marietta. Several blocks south, the road crosses Washington Street, after which it continues in conjunction with state Route 7, a primary highway that travels from Conneaut near Lake Erie all the

way to the state's southernmost point near Chesapeake on the Ohio River. Several more blocks pass as the road enters the downtown district, crossing Greene Street (mile 180), where Route 7 turns east and Route 26 begins, traveling north into Belmont County. Founded in 1788, Marietta is Ohio's oldest city, and today as the county seat it has a population of 14,500. Old 21 originally encountered the ramp to the Williamstown Bridge over the Ohio River (built in 1903 as a railway bridge) just south of Greene Street. That bridge was condemned in 1985, demolished, and rebuilt, reopening in 1991. The rebuilt ramp to the new bridge, however, begins three blocks to the east along Greene Street. Crossing this bridge ends the chapter of 21 in Ohio, taking the route into West Virginia.

(above left) Aerial view of the city in the early 1900s from a nearby hillside; the Muskingum River is in the foreground, with the Williamstown Bridge in the distance; (above right) Marietta's Williamstown Bridge under construction in 1903, complete with a traditional riverboat passing underneath; (middle right) View of the completed bridge, with its peculiarly assymetric shape; (right) The modern Williamstown Bridge opened in 1992 and by contrast, is totally symmetric; (below) View of Marietta skyline from the Williamstown Bridge.

U.S. Route 21 in West Virginia

Prior to the establishment of the U.S. Route system in 1926, the roads that would later make up Route 21 existed throughout West Virginia, in most cases as state routes. From Williamstown to Parkersburg, the road existed but was not numbered. From Parkersburg to Charleston, it was numbered as state Route 2, which was later rerouted to follow the Ohio River from Chester to Huntington. From Charleston to Chimney Corner, it was numbered as state Route 3, as well as being the Midland Trail and the Atlantic Pacific Highway. Today Route 3 covers a rural stretch of the southern part of the state. From Fayetteville to Bluefield, 21 was state Route 4, which today covers a rural stretch of the central part of the state.

Upon crossing the Williamstown Bridge (named for the town on the WV side, as WV technically owns and maintains the bridge), 21 enters Wood County of West Virginia, and from the bridge one can see the I-77 bridge over the Ohio River two miles east, straddling Buckley Island. Exiting the bridge as Highland Avenue, Old 21 officially enters West Virginia, the second of five states it travels through. Upon leaving the bridge, state Route 31 begins, going east to Harrisville in Ritchie County. Two blocks south, Old 21 turns right onto West 3rd Street, which is also the intersection with state Route 14, traveling from here south to Spencer in Roane County. U.S. 21 was decommissioned in West Virginia in 1974, three years after it lost its designation in Ohio, but before that it followed the current course of Route 14 from Williamstown to Mineral Wells, south of Parkersburg. The City of Williamstown has a population of just under 3,000 and is probably best known as the home of the Fenton Art Glass Company.

As Route 14 travels west out of town, it runs parallel to a main railroad line and within sight of the river for several miles. Quickly leaving Williamstown, the road becomes known as Williams Highway, and it soon passes through the unmarked locality of Pohick. At this point, the road's original alignment goes off to the right as Old River Road, returning to Route 14 approximately a mile later as the two roads go through the unincorporated residential communities of Sand Hill, Boaz, and Summit. Despite not being incorporated, Boaz is officially listed as a census-designated-place, and has a population of 1,345. Just beyond this is anoth-er unincorporated community, Central, south of which the road becomes Grand Central Avenue as it heads further south into the city of Vienna (population just under 11,000), at mile 190. Between 60th Street at the northern end of the city and 28th Street, the road is a boulevard with the lanes separated by a tree-lined strip of land. Beyond this it continues as a four-lane road, passing Grand Central Mall as it

(top right) Ohio River bridge as seen from Williamstown in the 1940s; (right) Skyline of Parkersburg, 1940s.

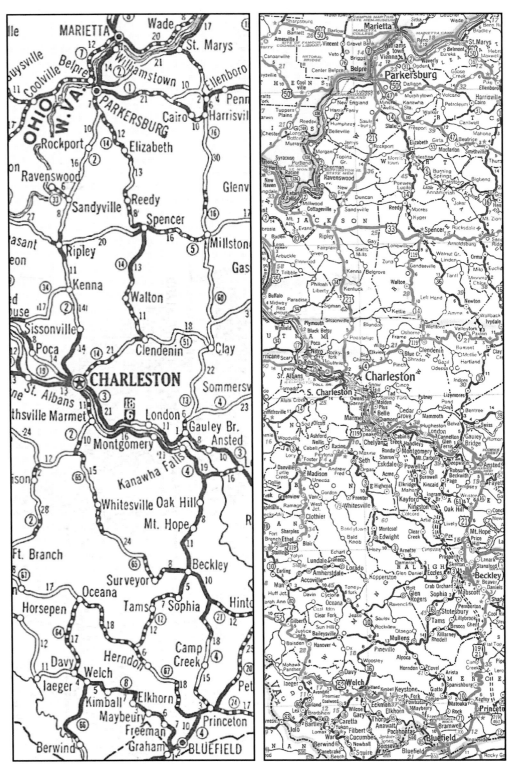

leaves Vienna and enters Parkersburg, at which time it becomes known as Murdoch Avenue.

Parkersburg (mile 195), with a population of just over 33,000, is the state's third-largest city and the Wood County seat. As Route 14/Old 21 continues south, it passes the Park Shopping Center in the locality of Beechwood. Just past this is the intersection with Emerson Avenue. A right turn (west) takes one to the Memorial Bridge over the river to Belpre, Ohio, while a left turn (east) takes

one onto state Route 68, which goes east a short distance to I-77. Route 68 then travels with Route 14/21 through Parkersburg, eventually continuing on to Ravenswood, further south on the river. From this point south, the original alignment of U.S. 21 followed Murdoch Avenue south into downtown, where it turned left (east) on 7th Street, which at the time was also U.S. Route 50, a major east-west route going from Ocean City, MD. west to San Francisco. Route 21 then traveled several blocks before turning right (south) on East Street, where it soon crossed a small toll bridge over the Little Kanawha River (which comes from the hills of eastern West Virginia and empties into the Ohio River just a mile west of here). Once on the other side of the river, (right) One of numerous motor courts along the road, this one with a Spanish theme, on the north side of Parkersburg; (below left) This new bridge over the Little Kanawha River allowed 21 to be rerouted in the 1940s on a more efficient course heading south out of Parkersburg; (bottom left and right) Two motels (the Sky Motel and Hiley's) along 21 on the city's south side in the early 1950s.

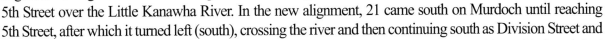

SPANISH TOURIST COURT
3815 MURDOCK AVE. (U. S. ROUTE 21) PARKERSBURG, W. VA.

MODERN CABINS - PRIVATE SHOWERS - INNERSPRING MATTRESSES
Mr. & Mrs. J. C. WARD

it was renamed as Pike Street, which continued south out of the city through South Parkersburg. In the 1940s, the alignment changed once a new bridge was built along 5th Street over the Little Kanawha River. In the new alignment, 21 came south on Murdoch until reaching 5th Street, after which it turned left (south), crossing the river and then continuing south as Division Street and later as Blizzard Street, eventually reuniting with the original alignment on Pike Street in South Parkersburg.

P-24 New Fifth Street Bridge and Little Kanawha River, Parkersburg, W. Va.

On State Route 2 and 14, U. S. 21

Today, following the course of Old 21 is a bit more challenging: state Route 14 follows its course for the most part, but has been rerouted somewhat in the city to improve traffic flow. Now, 14 splits into separate one-way northbound and southbound roads, just north of Emerson Avenue. Southbound, traffic on Murdoch travels west onto Ohio Avenue in front of the Park Shopping Center, and three blocks further south the traffic is routed further west to Garfield Avenue. This continues through downtown, past the Camden-Clark Memorial Hospital, until taking a sharp left turn south onto 4th Street. Four blocks later, it takes a quick left turn onto Green Street, followed by a right onto 5th Street (which is bidirectional south of this), which travels across the Little Kanawha River. Coming north, traffic on 5th Street continues to Juliana Street, where it takes a right (north) turn, going three blocks to 8th Street, where the route turns left, eventually curving into Murdoch Avenue in front of the hospital. At this point it has a brief intersection with state Route 618, a short road that covers the old alignment of U.S. 50 through the city (that route still existing but having been rerouted onto a modern highway on the south side of the Little Kanawha River).

SKYMOTEL
U. S. ROUTE #21 NORTH
PARKERSBURG, WEST VIRGINIA

Continuing south across the river, Division Street travels for several blocks in conjunction with state Route 95, another relatively short route within the city. Just south of this, Division becomes Blizzard Drive, which travels for a mile before connecting to Pike Street and leaving the city. Several miles later comes the

unincorporated community of Pettyville, at which point Route 14 follows a modern bypass of Pike Street for a mile as the road works its way down a hillside toward I-77. Old Pike Street winds its way down the hill just to the east of this, and the roads reconnect at the bottom. The road then crosses the interstate at exit 170 as it enters the unincorporated community of Mineralwells (mile 201), which as a census-designated-place has a

LIMESTONE HILL ON ROUTE No. 21 BETWEEN RIPLEY AND PARKERSBURG, W. VA.

(left) Limestone Hill, in northern Wirt County, as seen in the 1940s; (below left) Hillside barn painted with Kentucky Club Tobacco sign; made by the same company that made Mail Pouch Tobacco in Wheeling, WV., Kentucky Club was never advertised as heavily, although a few such barns have survived [photo taken in 1994 by Tim Murphy]; (below right) Covered bridge on Sarvis Fork Road, near Sandyville, as seen in 1985; (bottom left) Jackson County Courthouse in Ripley, circa 1940s; other than the clock tower now being painted white, it looks the same today; (bottom right) Vail Furniture in the center of Ripley, where it has been since 1844.

population of 1,860. Known as Elizabeth Pike at this point, the road splits just south of the community, with Route 14 continuing east and Old 21 traveling south as secondary state highway 21, also known as the Southern Highway. At one time a sign stood near this intersection, noting that it was "Old U.S. Route 21", but this is no longer in place. The road travels for several miles immediately parallel to the interstate, passing through the unincorporated locality of Saulsbury before passing under 77 yet again. The road then goes through the unincorporated community of Rockport (mile 210), consisting of a number of scattered houses along the road, before passing into Wirt County.

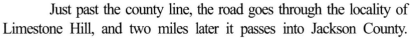
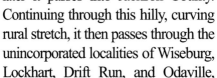

Just past the county line, the road goes through the locality of Limestone Hill, and two miles later it passes into Jackson County. Continuing through this hilly, curving rural stretch, it then passes through the unincorporated localities of Wiseburg, Lockhart, Drift Run, and Odaville, none consisting of more than a few scattered homes. Two miles past Odaville, a covered bridge (not an uncommon sight in Appalachia) can be seen just to the east of Old 21, on Sarvis Fork Road. Built in 1889, the bridge is 101 feet long, crosses the Left Fork of Sandy Creek, and is list-ed on the National Register of Historic Places. Another mile south, the road comes to the locality of New Era, which leads into the unincorporated

JACKSON COUNTY COURT HOUSE, RIPLEY, W. VA.

COMPLIMENTS - VILLAGE DAIRY STORE - A Good Place to Eat
Ripley, W. Va. - Interstate Rts. U.S. 21 and 33

(left) Ripley's Village Dairy Store, circa 1950; (below right) Shinn Service Station, as seen in 1994, along Old 21 just north of Kenna; although quaint, the visible register Gulf gas pump was not operational.

community of Sandyville (mile 225). Named after nearby Sandy Creek, the area has its own post office (zip code 25275), and has a population of more than 1,700 residents.

Seven miles further south through the countryside, the road comes to Ripley, the Jackson County seat, with a population of more than 3,200. Entering the city as North Church Street, Old 21 crosses the center of town at the intersection with Main Street (mile 232). Main Street is also U.S. Route 33, which originally traveled more

than 700 miles from Richmond, VA. west to St. Joseph, MI., although it now ends in Elkhart, IN. At the northeast corner of Main and Church Streets is Vail Furniture, a staple of the city since 1844, when Isaiah Vail opened a casket and furniture business. Still owned by Vail's descendents, the company continues to operate successfully after more than 165 years. From that same intersection, the Jackson County courthouse can be seen one block west on Court Street. 21 continues south out of the town as South Church Street, traveling four miles south before crossing under I-77 at Exit 132. Church Street is a bypass of the original alignment of U.S. 21, which turned left (east) one block south of Main Street onto Charleston Drive, which parallels Church Street for a mile before becoming Cedar Lane Drive. Once out of town, it is named on maps as Old U.S. 21 and follows a tortuous path up a long grade, going through the locality of Salt Hill before crossing under I-77 and entering the unincorporated community of Fairplain (mile 237),

where it reunites with the newer bypass road, which continues south. Although the official records are not conclusive, it appears that the bypass was built very soon after Route 21 was established in 1926.

Six miles beyond Fairplain, 21 comes to the unincorporated community of Kenna (mile 243), where it intersects state Route 34, which travels from here southwest to Hamlin, a small town west of Charleston. 21 then continues south through the unmarked localities of Young and Goldtown (mile 249), neither of which have much to distinguish them as communities. Just past this, the road crosses I-77 again at Exit 119, before continuing south, closely paralleling the interstate for the next three miles, including the unremarkable locality of Loop. The road then enters Kanawha County, the state's most populated county with 200,000 residents, and south of this, 21 is known as Sissonville Drive. The territory becomes

(above) Good's Motel, with its twenty modern units and attached Good's Restaurant, was located at 2380 Sissonville Drive, as seen circa 1960; (right) Skyline of Charleston, looking north across the Kanawha River.

Aerial View Kanawha River and Charleston, W. Va.

(left) Aerial view of Charleston, looking southeast along the Kanawha River; the main downtown area is in the center, with the state capitol in the distance, near the top of the picture; the mouth of the Elk River is in the foreground, and Route 21/60 passes through the area at the far left; (below left) Symbol for the Midland Trail [black stripe on orange background], seen on markers all along the route; (below right) Similar symbol for the Atlantic Pacific Highway, with black on yellow.

rockier, with more creeks and deeper valleys and hollows, as the road gets closer to the Kanawha River Valley. Being in the northern suburbs of Charleston at this point, the area gradually becomes more populous as well. After passing Exit 116 of the interstate, the road travels eastward away from the highway, into the unincorporated but census-designated-place of Sissonville (mile 255), situated along the Pocatalico River, with a population of 4,400. The road then heads back to the interstate, crossing under it at Exit 114; at this point the road is briefly numbered as state Route 622, which travels from this point south to the town of Institute, along the Kanawha River. The road then continues through the unincorporated communities of White Chapel, Pocatalico, and Guthrie (mile 264), before it finally enters the city of Charleston.

Established as a city in 1794, Charleston is the state capitol (one of two that Route 21 passes through, Columbia, South Carolina being the other), the Kanawha County Seat, and the largest city in West Virginia, with an estimated population of 50,300 as of 2008, and a metropolitan area with a total population of just over 300,000 residents. Most of the city lies in the relatively narrow Kanawha River Valley, near its intersection with the Elk River, and much of its industrial base can be seen traveling southeast through the valley, with numerous chemical and power plants and other factories, as well as various aspects of the coal industry visible along the way. The Kanawha River begins at Gauley Bridge from the union of the New and Gauley Rivers, draining much of eastern West Virginia, western Virginia, and western North Carolina. The river then

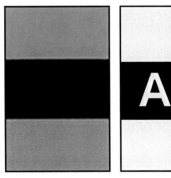

travels nearly sixty miles northwest from Charleston, joining the Ohio River at Point Pleasant.

As Sissonville Drive curves its way down into the valley, it almost immediately goes from a mountainous rural/suburban setting to a setting of inner-city housing projects upon its intersection with Washington Street West, where Sissonville Road and secondary state Route 21 both end at the intersection of U.S. Route 60. Old 21 turned left (southeast) here and ran in conjunction with 60 for the next 45 miles, all of it within the Kanawha and New River Valley. U.S. 60 is a major east-west federal route, stretching in its original course nearly 3,000 miles from Virginia Beach, VA. to central Los Angeles, although today it ends in western Arizona.

Much of Route 60 in the east follows the transcontinental Midland Trail and Atlantic Pacific Highway, two of the country's original Auto Trails that were established around 1913. The road itself, however, dates to the early 1800s, as it paralleled the New and Kanawha Rivers, which made it a preferred pathway for settlers and travelers moving west through the region. Some structures from the early Nineteenth Century still stand along the road today.

Daniel Boone Hotel in the 1950s

The Daniel Boone

In beautiful West Virginia, the Switzerland of America. Attractive 11 story, fire proof hotel was erected by the citizens of Charleston, W.Va., at a cost of two and one-half million dollars in memory of Daniel Boone, famous pioneer and scout of nearly 200 years ago. Located in the center of the city and just a short distance from the State Capitol. 465 rooms, each with bath, circulating ice water and radio loud speaker. 214 rooms and all public space completely air conditioned. You will like the homelike atmosphere of the Daniel Boone.

ROGER S. CREEL
Managing Director

THE NEW KANAWHA VALLEY BANK BUILDING, CHARLESTON. W. VA.

(left) **Kanawha Valley Building when it was new in the 1930s; (above) Clay Center for the Arts and Sciences; (below) West Virginia State Capitol Building, as seen from Kanawha Boulevard; (bottom left) Governor's Mansion, literally next door to the capitol building, as seen in the 1950s.**

Originally, Washington Street carried Routes 21 and 60 throughout the city. Today, Route 60 travels approximately one mile east of Sissonville Drive before splitting into two parallel one-way roads: Washington Street takes the westbound traffic, while Lee Street takes the eastbound traffic toward town. Several blocks after this, the roads cross Pennsylvania Avenue South, numbered as U.S. Route 119, which travels nearly 600 miles from DuBois, PA. to Pineville, KY. Immediately after this, the roads cross under Interstate 64, which travels nearly 1,000 miles from Chesapeake, VA. to Wentzville, MO., west of St. Louis. Both roads soon cross separate bridges over the Elk River (which travels more than 170 miles from the mountains of eastern WV to the Kanawha River several blocks south of this point) and into the downtown district (mile 270).

Just after crossing the river, Lee Street passes the Charleston Civic Center, completed in 1959, which includes a large convention facility and a 13,000 seat arena. Just past this is the Charleston Town Center Mall, a huge three-story shopping complex that opened in 1983, also facing Lee Street. Across from this, between Lee and Washington Streets, stand the Charleston Marriott and Embassy Suites hotels. Just beyond this is the 18-story glass covered Laidley Tower, a modern office building that is one of the city's tallest structures. Across from this, on the north side of Washington Street, is the St. Francis Hospital complex. Two blocks further along, at the northeast corner of Washington and Capitol Streets, is the former Daniel Boone Hotel, standing eleven stories tall and on the National Register of Historic Places. Opened in 1929, it once had 465 rooms, but after closing it was renovated into an office building, which remains open today. In the next block, the

Kanawha Valley Building stands at the corner of Lee and Capitol Streets. Completed in 1929, it is the city's only true "skyscraper" at 22 stories and 265 feet in height, being the city's second tallest building after the state capitol. Two blocks further east, standing between Lee and Washington, is the Clay Center for the Arts and Sciences, which opened in 2003. Consisting of a performance hall with nearly 1,900 seats, a theater, and the Avampato Discovery Museum featuring both scientific exhibits and an art gallery, the Clay Center is one of the most ambitious cultural entities in the country. On the far side of the Clay

Governor's Mansion, Charleston, West Virginia

Kanawha Boulevard from Kanawha City Bridge showing Capitol Dome, Charleston, W. Va.

(left) Kanawha Boulevard looking west along the river toward the capitol in the 1940s; the street remains residential today; (below) Motel in Riverview, circa 1950.

Center, Route 60 eastbound leaves Lee Street, turning left on Brooks Street for one block to continue back to Washington Street, which then returns to two-way traffic. On the north side of Washington at this point is the Charleston Area Medical Center (CAMC, the state's largest hospital system), General Hospital campus. Continuing east, Route 60 then leaves the heart of downtown, continuing east one mile before reaching the state capitol complex.

Upon reaching Greenbrier Street (numbered as state Route 114, which travels several miles north to the community of Big Chimney), Washington Street temporarily ends at the capitol plaza. Washington originally continued straight here, but has since been incorporated into the plaza for pedestrian use only. At this point, access to I-77 at Exit 99 is just one block north on Greenbrier. Route 60 turns right (south) one block to Kanawha Boulevard East,

Located on Kanawha Blvd., ½ Mile East of Charleston City Limits on U. S. Highways 60 & 21 (Post Office Address: Riverview, W. Va.)

where it then turns left to continue east along the river and past the capitol building. The West Virginia State Capitol building itself is a majestic limestone structure topped with an ornate dome, which at 292 feet in height is the state's tallest structure. The entire dome is gilded in 14-karat gold leaf applied to the copper and lead roof in small squares. Built at a cost of $10 million, the building was dedicated in 1932, and it is surrounded by several other government buildings and fountains in the capitol plaza. The Governor's Mansion, built in 1925, is a Georgian Revival building that stands immediately to the west of the capitol building.

As Route 60 continues east along Kanawha Boulevard, it passes a pleasant, older residential neighborhood of large houses, before passing under the twin bridges for 35th and 36th Streets. The road soon passes out of the city of Charleston at a locality known as Riverview. East of this, the road runs directly parallel to I-77 (which is in conjunction with I-64 in this stretch), as the roads pass through a narrow strip of land between the river and a steep cliff that rises straight up from the river level. Following old Routes 21/60 becomes difficult again in another mile, as Kanawha Blvd. ends on an entrance ramp onto I-64/77, with the

(below) Two views of the Dupont Company's Belle chemical plant in the 1970s; in the left image, Routes 21/60 pass to the right, at the base of the hill.

(left) Coal barge passing through the Marmet Locks on the Kanawha River; (below) Aerial view of the American Electric Power plant in Glasgow, WV.; (bottom left) Views of the London Locks on the Kanawha River in the 1940s and today as seen from Routes 21/60.

interstate carrying Route 60 for the next mile through the locality of Snow Hill, while the original alignment of the road can be seen immediately to the north, at the base of the cliff, as Piedmont Road. 60 then exits the interstate to continue east on Kanawha Blvd., which is now a four-lane divided highway, while the interstate starts a large sweeping turn which carries it onto the Chuck Yeager Bridge over the river, after which it becomes the West Virginia Turnpike. Route 60 then passes under the bridge and into a small unincorporated community known at different times as Reed and now Port Amherst. The original alignment disappears for the next half-mile, the highway having been built over it, although it soon appears again as Malden Drive, now on the south/west side of the modern road. Malden Drive soon curves toward the river, with Midland Drive branching off to continue on as old Route 21/60. As the road runs parallel to the Kanawha River, it runs east, southeast, or directly south in different stretches. In this particular stretch the road is traveling due south.

Both Kanawha Blvd. and Midland Drive then pass through the unincorporated but sizeable community of Rand. It then continues into the unincorporated community of Dupont City (this general area is also known variously as Malden or Lower Belle), at which time it is

renamed as W. Dupont Avenue. This area was established as a neighborhood for workers at the huge DuPont Company's Belle chemical plant that stands between the road and the river. Opened in 1925, the complex covers nearly 700 acres and at its peak in the 1950s employed over 5,000 workers. Employing around 500 people today, it produces numerous commercial chemicals such as agricultural herbicides and fungicides, and acrylics for paint and plastics. Just down river from the plant is the Marmet Locks and Dam along the river, opened in 1934 and named for the town just across the river at this point. Its river traffic consisting almost entirely of coal barges, it is one of numerous sets of locks along the river's course, and is visible from the road. Back on Route 60, the road soon passes into the town of Belle (mile 280), with its population of 1,250. While the road continues as a four-lane divided highway, the original alignment of 21/60 can be seen immediately to the left

Government Dam and Lock on Kanawha River between Charleston and Montgomery, W. Va.

45

(left) Aerial view of the Mammoth Coal Co. mine near Smithers, with Routes 21/60 passing through the site; (below) Motel in Smithers as seen in the 1950s; (below left) One of numerous small coal mines in the area around Boomer in the early 1900s.

(north) in two brief stretches, as Midland Drive and Old U.S. 60. The road then crosses Witcher Creek and into the unincorporated community of Diamond before continuing east, soon passing the modern Admiral Lopez Bridge over the river to the town of Cabin Creek. I-64/77 runs parallel to 21/60 on the south side of the river from Charleston to this point, although east of this, the interstate turns south to ascend into the hills.

Most of the original alignment of 21/60 has been built over by the current road through this stretch, and upon reaching the next community, Shrewsbury (mile

285), the road narrows to two lanes and largely follows the road's original course beyond that. At that point the road name briefly reverts from Midland Trail back to East Dupont Avenue. Passing the unmarked and unremarkable locality of Monarch, the road then comes to the town of Cedar Grove, population 862. This is the site of Fort Kelley, the valley's oldest settlement, dating to 1773. Here, the road's original alignment can be seen as an exit ramp into the town, curving back under the new road and into town as Main Street, before curving back to rejoin the current road on the east side of town. Nearly adjacent to Cedar Grove is the town of Glasgow (mile 289) with its population of 783. Immediately past the town and along the river is a large coal-fired power plant, opened in 1952 and operated by the Appalachian Power Co., a division of the American Electric Power Co. Continuing east, the road passes through the locality of Riverside and the unincorporated communities of Hugheston and London (mile 293). In the latter area, the road's original alignment can be seen briefly for several blocks just to the east of the current road. Also at London is the uppermost set of locks along the Kanawha River, built in 1930 and visible from the highway.

Beyond the locks, the road travels through the site

(right) The huge West Virginia Alloys Co. plant in Alloy, as seen from Route 60 and from the river.

(left) Falls View, a company town built for employees of the nearby alloy plant, with Route 60 in the foreground; (below) One of several small waterfalls cascading down the cliffs on the north side of Route 60 in this area.

of a huge coal mining facility, run by the Mammoth Coal Company, a division of the Massey Energy Company. At the road level, all that is visible are the main buildings of the facility and a huge bank of coal waiting to be transported away via river barge. What isn't seen is the enormous coal recovery operation existing at the top of the nearby hills immediately north of the road, covering hundreds of acres and which is the source of the coal that is piled at the riverside. This is just one of many coal mines still operating in West Virginia, yet it is the only one that is still visible along the entire course of Route 21. In particular, this area along the river was once rich with coal mining. Just beyond the mine site is a bridge crossing the river to the town of Montgomery, and immediately past this is the Fayette County line. The city of Smithers (mile 297) is just past the line, with the associated localities of Carbondale and Cannelton, the entire area having a population of just over 900. Continuing east, the road passes through the locality of Longacre before reaching the unincorporated community of Boomer, another area

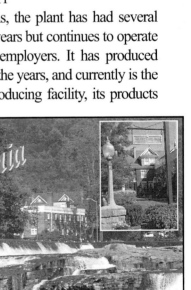

built around coal mining. Just past the town, in the locality of Alloy, is the huge plant of the West Virginia Alloys Company. Built in 1911 with many subsequent additions, the plant has had several changes in ownership over the years but continues to operate as one of the region's largest employers. It has produced numerous alloy metals through the years, and currently is the world's largest silicon metal producing facility, its products

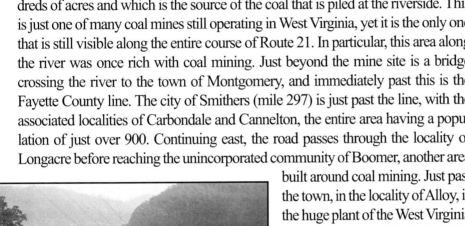

being used heavily in the computer chip industry. Beyond this is the locality of Falls View (mile 302), a company town (like several communities along the river) built around 1930 for employees of the nearby alloy plant. Next is the unincorporated residential community of Charlton Heights. By this time, the

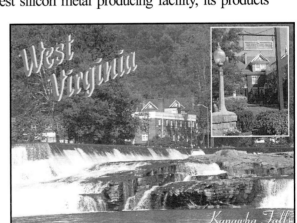

(above) View of Kanawha Falls in the 1930s, when the power plant was still in operation; (right) Close-up view of the falls, with the Glen Ferris Inn in the background; (below) Wide-angle view of the falls, with the old power station at far left [photo by Ken Thomas].

(left) Glen Ferris Inn as it appeared in 2000; (below) Postcard view of the Gauley Bridge area, showing the Gauley River entering from the left to join the New River, seen in the distance, to form the Kanawha River in the foreground.

river valley has become considerably narrower and deeper, with the surrounding landscape more mountainous and filled with beautiful scenery. Several different streams create small waterfalls (especially prominent in the spring) over the cliff on the north side of the road through this stretch. Nevertheless, as the region becomes less and less populated, it has an oddly detached and isolated feel, not unlike various other rural areas of Route 21. Just ahead, another small bridge crosses the river to a now sparsely populated south side, while the road approaches Kanawha Falls.

With a drop of only fifteen feet, Kanawha Falls is not one of the more spectacular waterfalls, yet the width of the river and the surrounding hillsides make the area very photogenic and popular with tourists. A small park along Route 60 just below the falls allows excellent views as well as access to the river for fishing, boating, and just wading. A dam exists just above the falls to divert water toward the old abandoned hydroelectric station that stands on the far north side of the falls. Just west of the falls is

View of Gauley Bridge, W. Va. on U. S. 60, Showing Junction of Gauley and New Rivers   7A-H3932

MIDLAND TRAIL BRIDGE, GAULEY BRIDGE, W. VA.

(above) View from the Gauley Bridge area looking west toward Glen Ferris; some of the state's most photographed scenery is in this region; (above left) View of the original Route 21/60 bridge [on the right] over the Gauley River, next to the main railroad bridge [on the left]; (left) Today the railroad bridge remains standing, although the Route 60 bridge has long since been razed [although its supports remain] in favor of the current bridge which runs just to the south of the old one; in this view, one can just barely see in the background the supports of the original toll bridge that was destroyed during the Civil War.

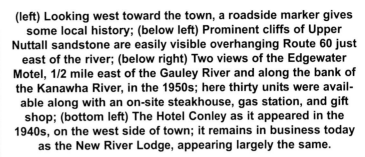

(left) Looking west toward the town, a roadside marker gives some local history; (below left) Prominent cliffs of Upper Nuttall sandstone are easily visible overhanging Route 60 just east of the river; (below right) Two views of the Edgewater Motel, 1/2 mile east of the Gauley River and along the bank of the Kanawha River, in the 1950s; here thirty units were available along with an on-site steakhouse, gas station, and gift shop; (bottom left) The Hotel Conley as it appeared in the 1940s, on the west side of town; it remains in business today as the New River Lodge, appearing largely the same.

historically the site of a ferry that operated until 1927, forming a crucial part of the road south from the area. Traffic going south from the Midland Trail had to cross the river at this site in order to access a steep, twisting road out of the valley on the south side of the river. This road today is secondary state Route 13, and follows the original route to the village of Beckwith, where it connects with Old 21. Once the federal route system was put into place, traffic began to increase through the area, and the original ferry quickly became inadequate. At times of high water, crossing the river could involve a wait of an hour or two. By the spring of 1927, two ferries were being used, each carrying four to five cars and taking five minutes to load or unload, and three minutes to cross the river. It was estimated that over 1,700 cars could be carried daily in this manner, although this still would prove to be inadequate. Once the connection from Chimney Corner to Beckwith several miles east of here was completed in late 1927 (involving the construction of a road down Cotton Hill and a bridge crossing the New River), the ferry became obsolete and was eventually phased out, along with the construction of the bridge just west of here. It was at this time that signs for Route 21 were put in place through Gauley Bridge and beyond, as one of the last remaining sections of the route through the state was finished.

Just beyond the falls is the unincorporated village of Glen Ferris, with an estimated population of 200. The most well-known busi-

ness in the village is the Glen Ferris Inn, built around 1810 as a residence for Colonel Aaron Stockton, a local businessman and grandson of a signer of the Declaration of Independence. In 1839, the home was opened as a hotel for travelers, and continued as Stockton's Inn until being purchased by Union Carbide (which operated a nearby aluminum plant and built many of the homes in the village) in the 1920s for use as a hotel

(left) Cathedral Falls, just east of Gauley Bridge; (bottom) View of the New River Valley from Gauley Mountain; the full view is often obscured by mist.

for guests of the company. At that time the hotel was enlarged with a modern addition, giving it fifteen guest rooms. Since 1996 it has been owned by local residents and remains open today, as well as being listed on the National Register of Historic Places.

After another mile, the road curves into the town of Gauley Bridge (mile 307), with its population of 738. Named after the Gauley River and a railroad bridge that crossed it in the mid-1800s, the town was first explored in 1671, when Captain Thomas Batts discovered and claimed the area for King Charles II of England and Ireland. Nearly two centuries later the area was sparsely settled, but an early railroad bridge existed across the river in what is now the town of Gauley Bridge. In September 1861, in the early days of the Civil War, Union General W.S. Rosecrans defeated Confederate General John B. Floyd at Carnifex Ferry, approximately twenty miles to the east, a victory that assured Union control of western Virginia. The original toll bridge across the Gauley was destroyed by retreating Confederates at that time, although the stone piers can still be seen just north of the current railroad bridge. The original Route 60 steel arch bridge across the river was immediately south of the current railroad bridge, although it has since been replaced by a more modern bridge just to the south of that. The Gauley River begins in the mountains of eastern West Virginia and follows a winding course to this point, where it joins the New River to form the Kanawha River. The Gauley is best known for the whitewater rafting that takes place along its course, with numerous Class IV and V (the most dangerous) rapids that attract thousands of adventurers from all over the world. At Gauley Bridge, Route 60 intersects state Routes 16 (traveling from St. Marys on the Ohio River to McDowell on the Virginia state line) and 39 (traveling along much of the former path of U.S. Route 19 from this point east to the Virginia state line in Pocahontas County). The original course of U.S. Route 19 came through the town on its way south, before traveling concurrently with U.S. 21 all the way to Bluefield. In later years Route 19 was routed east onto the Mountaineer Expressway, joining former Route 21 just north of Beckley.

Gauley Bridge is near the site of one of the worst industrial disasters in American history, the Hawks Nest Incident. In 1927, Union Carbide decided to use the New River to create power for its ferroalloy plant several miles downriver at Alloy, and it contracted to have a dam and power plant built at Hawks Nest several miles up the river from Gauley Bridge. This dam would divert water into a tunnel which ran three miles under Gauley Mountain, re-entering the river near Gauley Bridge.

The dam and old power plant at Glen Ferris were also part of this project. Nearly 3,000 workers were recruited for the project from all over the south, many of them African-Americans desperate for work. In the process of building the tunnel, the mineral silica was discovered, and in the process of blasting away rock, a tremendous amount of silica dust filled the air. The workers were without masks, and many subsequently developed silicosis, an essentially terminal lung dis-

(left) The Chimney Corner Gift Shop and motor court as seen in the 1940s; earlier postcards show the main log cabin as a solitary residence; several buildings had been added to the complex by the 1950s, although those are all gone today; (below left) The original log cabin remains at the site [as shown in 2000] today, still housing a gift shop.

ease. Workers gradually died over the coming years, with the company eventually admitting to just over 100 deaths. A later Congressional hearing placed the toll at 476, while other estimates tended to suggest closer to 700 deaths. The majority of these were African-Americans who had largely been given the more dangerous work in the tunnels due to discrimination. If nothing else, the incident helped lead to better understanding of silicosis, although it was more than a decade later before the condition could be claimed for workman's compensation.

Back on the road, as Route 60 leaves town, it passes the New River Campground, owned by the WV Chapter of the Paralyzed Veterans of America. Shortly after this is one of the more impressive sites along the entire length of Old 21: the appropriately named Cathedral Falls. Set in a narrow and deep hollow on the north side of the road, the falls is created by the Cane Branch stream which falls more than 100 feet over multiple ledges of Upper Nuttall sandstone, creating a spectacular view. The falls has a parking lot and picnic shelter nearby, and the base is easily accessible to visitors. Climbing beside the falls, one is able to actually walk behind them in certain areas. Continuing east, the road soon reaches the locality of Gauley Junction, named for a railroad bridge across the New River which joins a main line on the south

side, although this is no longer visible from the road due to overgrowth of trees. The road then gradually begins to climb out of the valley as it ascends Gauley Mountain. Near the top, the Hawks Nest State Park Golf Course appears unexpectedly, and past that is a scenic overlook with room to pull over to view the river valley. Gauley Mountain is a ridge, the peak of which reaches 2,539 feet

The Old Man of the Canyon on Route 19 and 21 near Chimney Corner, New River, W. Va.

(right) Unique rock formation at the entrance to the bridge over the New River; (below) View from the bridge level looking up Cotton Hill, circa early 1930s; note the primitive paving and the lack of guardrails and lane markers.

SCENE ON ROUTE 21 NEAR COTTON HILL W.Va.

(left) Original Route 21 bridge across the New River; (below left) Current bridge, after being rebuilt in the 1990s; (below right) Two views of scenic Laurel Creek, flowing along side of Route 21 south of the river, near Beckwith; in the lower photo, again note the early paving and lack of safety features.

above sea level, several miles east near Ansted. Along Route 60 the road ascends 1,000 feet over two miles before beginning a gradual, winding descent, and after a particularly sharp hairpin turn, the road arrives at Chimney Corner (mile 311).

Chimney Corner is an unincorporated locality that is unremarkable aside from sitting at the junction of U.S. 60 and state Route 16, which is former U.S. 19 and 21. At this point, 60 turns left to continue east through a series of tight curves to Hawks Nest State Park and overlook, on its way to Lewisburg and into Virginia. At the intersection is a log cabin that was once a residence, but by the late 1940s had been converted into a motor court. Today it houses a gift shop, with the Chimney Corner Cafe across the road, sitting along the bank of the Big Creek. From this point, Route 16 travels directly south, parallel to 60 for the next mile, while it descends quickly down Cotton Hill into the New River Valley. It was this section of road, from here to Beckwith, that was built in 1927 to complete Route 21 through the region. Also known as the New River Gorge, the valley is sometimes referred to as the Grand Canyon of the East (although there are other locations that have that nickname as well). Despite its name, the New River is often thought to be the oldest river in North America, anywhere from 10 million to 360 million years old. Known large-

ly for the extensive whitewater rafting that takes place in its gorge, the river begins in far northwestern North Carolina, flowing on a generally northward course through Virginia and into West Virginia, where it joins the Gauley to form the Kanawha River, eventually draining into the Ohio River. Once Route 16/Old 21 crosses the New River, it

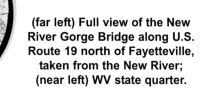

(far left) Full view of the New River Gorge Bridge along U.S. Route 19 north of Fayetteville, taken from the New River; (near left) WV state quarter.

(left) Fayette County courthouse, built in 1897; the building is on the National Register of Historic Places; (below) Yeager's Chuck Wagon Motel and Restaurant on Routes 21/16 between Fayetteville and Oak Hill.

continues south and begins to ascend the hill on the far side, paralleling the small but scenic Laurel Creek on the west side of the road. Passing through the unincorporated community of Beckwith, the road then turns east, passing through the unmarked localities of Youngstown, Bachman, and Oak Ridge before reaching the outskirts of Fayetteville (mile 319), the county seat.

Prior to reaching the town, Route 16 crosses the Mountaineer Expressway (current U.S. Route 19), which parallels the road from this point south to Beckley. This road is also known as Corridor L of the Appalachian Development Highway System. Going just one mile north on the expressway takes one over the famed New River Gorge Bridge, opened in 1977. At a height of 876 feet, this is the world's second-highest vehicular bridge, and at a length of just over 3,000 feet, it was until recently the longest single-arched steel bridge in the world. It is closed for one day every October, known as "Bridge Day," when people come from all over the world to walk across the bridge and take part in rappelling and BASE jumping. The bridge is famous enough that it was used as a primary symbol of West Virginia on the 2005 state quarter. U.S. Route 19 is one of the country's longest north-south federal highways, traveling more than 1,400 miles from Erie, PA. south to the Bradenton, FL. area, and a lengthy portion of the road is shared with Old 21 in West Virginia.

Fayetteville itself has a population of over 2,700 and is named for Marquis de Lafayette, the Frenchman who was a hero of both the American and French Revolutions. Entering the town on North Court Street, Route 16 passes the county courthouse, built in 1897, before curving south and quickly out of the town. Continuing south, the road passes through the locality of Fayette Heights two miles later, before Route 16 turns right onto Appalachian Drive, to again meet up with the expressway. The road's original alignment was straight onto what is now a dead end street, as its original course was built over by the highway. Route 16 now follows the expressway for a mile before exiting at East Main Street to continue south.

(above left) Main Street in Oak Hill in the 1950s; (below left) Hotel Hill on West Main Street in the center of town, circa early 1960s; the building remains standing today, occupied by offices and apartments; (right) WOAY is the area's ABC television affiliate, with studios along Route 16 on the south side of Oak Hill since the 1950s.

4

WOAY-TV

At that point, a short section of the original alignment going north is visible as Old Fayetteville Road.

East Main Street then enters the town of Oak Hill, traveling initially through the locality of East Oak Hill. Oak Hill has a population of nearly 7,600 and is the largest town along the road between Charleston and Beckley. The town is essentially split in half by the expressway, and after East Main Street passes under that, it enters the main business district (mile 325). After passing Central Avenue, the road becomes West Main Street, and after passing Jones Avenue, it is joined by state Route 61, which shares the road from here to Mount Hope on its way from downtown Charleston south to Piney View in Raleigh County. Once West Main Street travels out of town, it soon meets up again with the expressway, which covers the original road at this point. Routes 16/61 enter the expressway for a brief stretch before exiting again, onto Pea Ridge Road, in the locality of Greenstown. Here the road passes the studios and antennas for WOAY Television, the local ABC affiliate. On the air since 1954, the station was carried for many years on local channel 4, until ending its analog transmission in 2009; its digital transmission is still carried on local channel 50. Interestingly, the station's call let-

ters were originally intended to be WOAK (for obvious reasons), but the handwritten application was misread in the early 1950s, and the current letters were assigned at that time.

Continuing south, the road passes through the unincorporated community of Hilltop before reaching the larger but still unincorporated community of Glen Jean (mile 329). A boom town in the 1870s, the town had a major railroad junction and its economy was based on the local coal industry, flourishing to the point where it had its own opera house, hotels, and a company store. Little remains from that era, although the Bank of Glen Jean building remains standing today, just a block off the main road. In operation from 1909 to 1939, the bank was the financial center of local coal and railroad operations under the control of William McKell, whose mother Jean was the town's namesake. The building

(above) Main Street in Mount Hope, circa 1912; many of these buildings still stand today; (right) Advertisement for Samuel Dixon's White Oak Coal Co., one of the town's many such operations in the 1920s and part of the New River Company.

(left) Former headquarters of the New River Co. in Mount Hope as it appears today; the building is on the National Register of Historic Places; (below left) Another New River building, originally used as the company store and later as a garage; (below) One of the town's oldest standing structures, the First National Bank of Mount Hope was built in 1917 and still stands along Main Street, in use as a medical clinic.

is listed today in the National Register of Historic Places. Continuing south, the road continues through the unmarked localities of Derryhale and Dunloup before reaching the city of Mount Hope (mile 332), with a population of nearly 1,500. Just north of the town, Routes 16/61 intersect state Route 211, which is the original alignment of U.S. 21 through the town, following a much older stage coach line. While Routes 16/61 bypass the town on its east side, through the localities of Turkey Knob and McDonald (where Route 61 breaks off to travel southeast), Route 211 enters the town as Main Street, jogging one block to the west at

Mountain Avenue to continue as Main Street.

Mount Hope was another coal boom town, growing rapidly after the first mines opened in the 1890s, such that by the 1920s, there were an amazing twenty different coal companies with headquarters in and around the town. By that time, with all of the workers in coal camps and their families, the population of the surrounding area was as high as 30,000 at any given time. By the 1950s, however, the area had peaked and began a gradual decline that largely ended in the 1980s, when the last of the local coal companies (the New River Co.) closed. The largest of the local coal companies since its founding in 1906 by Englishman Samuel Dixon, New River's headquarters and two other buildings still

(right) Postcard view of Bailey's Motor Court in Bradley, with its fourteen units, circa 1950; (below) Local advertisements from the 1950s for establishments along Routes 19 and 21 in Beckley; the Green Bank Motel remains in business today.

(left) Aerial view of Beckley's central business district, looking east in the 1950s; (below) Hotel Beckley, at the southwest corner of South Kanawha and Main Streets; used as an office building today, the rear portions have been razed and the building is an off-white color.

stand along Main Street today. While most evidence of the coal industry's history is gone from the area, many buildings from the previous century still stand in Mount Hope. One of those along Main Street was built in 1910 as a clubhouse for employees of the New River Co., then was converted into the Mount Hope Hotel in 1921, and six years later was renamed as the New River Hotel. In 1931, it was upgraded and reopened as the Mountainair Hotel, remaining in business for many years. Although vacant now, it still stands at Main Street and North Mountain Avenue. Also of note are the Bon-Bon store, in business since 1920 selling confectionery and hardware, still owned by the son of the founder, and the abandoned Mt. Hope movie theater on the town's south side.

On the far side of the town, Route 211 ends at the junction with the Route 16 bypass. Just a mile later, the road passes into Raleigh County and the locality of Price Hill. At this point the road is marked as Robert C. Byrd Drive, named after the senator who served in Congress from 1959 to 2010, making him the longest-serving congressman in the country's history. The road then passes under the Mountaineer Expressway before passing through the unincorporated community of Bradley (mile

335), which is listed as a census-designated-place with a population of nearly 2,400. The village was officially given a title in the 1940s when it requested its own post office, and was named after General Omar Bradley.

Just past Bradley, the road travels back under the expressway, at which point U.S. 19 exits the expressway to travel in conjunction with Old 21 for the rest of the way to Bluefield. Just past this on the west side of the road is the Crossroads Mall, the area's largest, opened in 1981. Now in the greater Beckley area, the road passes through the localities of Prosperity and Cranberry before entering the city proper, at the site of the Beckley Plaza Shopping Center. Just past Cranberry, Market Road veers off to the right, traveling east of the road and on the far side of the shopping center for approximately one mile before rejoining Robert C. Byrd Drive in Skelton. This is a section of the original alignment of U.S. 19/21 and it still appears as such on some current maps.

Beckley is the seat of Raleigh County with a pop-

(left) King Tut Drive-In as it appeared in the 1940s and today, along Eisenhower Drive.

(left) Two views of the Honey In The Rock Motel, in 1962 and 2001, at the intersection of Route 19/Old 21 and South Fayette Street; named for the Civil War-themed outdoor play of the same name that has been performed annually since 1961 at nearby Grandview Park (hence the cannon at the top of the motel's sign), the hotel changed ownership in recent years and is now known as Wellspring Inn & Suites.

ulation of more than 16,800, making it the state's eighth-largest city, although the greater metropolitan area has nearly 80,000 residents. Just beyond the shopping center in the locality of Skelton, Route 19/Old 21 bears to the left onto North Eisenhower Drive as a bypass of downtown, built in the 1940s, while Robert C. Byrd Drive (and state Route 16) bears to the right as the original route through the city. Following the latter route, it travels through the locality of Sprague on the outskirts of town before reaching the intersection with state Route 210, which represents the original course of U.S. 21. Turning left onto this

road leaves Route 16 behind, and the scenery gradually goes from residential to commercial as downtown Beckley approaches. Crossing Main Street (mile 339) is the unofficial center of town, at which point the road becomes South Kanawha Street. At this intersection is the building once occupied by the Hotel Beckley, and across the street from that is the studio for radio station WJLS. After passing the central business district, the road quickly returns to a suburban residential setting over the next two miles before descending a gradual hill to rejoin Route 19/Eisenhower Drive, as Route 210 ends.

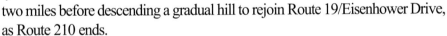

Returning to the Eisenhower Drive bypass route, it maintains a heavy commercial setting along its entire length of just over three miles, one that has continued to grow rapidly in recent years. The resulting traffic issues have led to the creation of a new bypass, to be built in sections and known as the "Z-Way," which would travel further east of the city to relieve much of the congestion. After passing the Beckley Crossing and other shopping centers in the Skelton area, the traffic lightens somewhat as the road continues south. Ironically, there is a Rue 21 clothing store in the Cranberry Creek Plaza; as a national chain, it has no connection to the road's original name, even though it

(left) Advertisement for a local restaurant and gas station in the 1950s; (above) The Moon Glo Motel opened in Beaver in the early 1950s and still remains open today, operating as the Patriot Inn. The neon sign was one of the most ornate along the entire course of Route 21 but is no longer standing; unfortunately there are no known photos of it lighted at night. Earlier images of the sign do not show the satellite at the top, suggesting that it was added some time after the "Space Race" of the late 1950s.

means "Route 21" or "21 Road" in French. Soon after this comes the intersection with Stanaford Road, carrying state Route 41. U.S. 19 had originally joined 21 at Gauley Bridge, thirty miles to the north, but in the 1940s was routed further east to join 21 at this point. Once the Mountaineer Expressway was completed in the late 1970s, Route 19 was realigned yet again to that road, with Route 41 taking its previous alignment from Sutton to Beckley. Route 41 follows Eisenhower Drive for a mile before turning west on Johnstown Road and heading into town. One mile further south is a connection to the previously mentioned "Z-Way," which travels south to Interstate 64. Beyond this, Route 19 begins to descend into the valley of Piney Creek, a New River tributary that parallels the road for several miles. After passing South Kanawha Drive/Route 210/original 21, the road intersects South Fayette Street and state Route 3, which travels nearly 200 miles through mountainous southern West Virginia and which shares the road for the next six miles to Shady Spring. Just past this are the unincorporated localities of Raleigh and Glen Morgan, after which the road is known as Ritter Drive as it passes through the valley and under the high bridge for Interstate 64.

Continuing through the Piney Creek Valley, the road passes through the unincorporated community known variously as Beaver or Blue Jay (mile 344). The name Blue Jay comes from the Blue Jay Lumber Company which operated in the area in the 1930s, with a narrow gauge railroad that traveled through the area from here south to Mercer County, where a great deal of logging was taking place. In the Beaver/Blue Jay area is the intersection with state Route 307, which travels east before looping back to rejoin Routes 19/21 approximately four miles south of this point. One mile south of Beaver is the community of Daniels, which

is listed as a census-designated place with a population of more than 1,800. Just south of Daniels, a narrow road looking more like a driveway veers off to the right; marked as Mathis Road, this is one of several places in the area where the road's original alignment can be seen. Traveling parallel to Route 19/21, it crosses the road approximately a mile south and continues on the east side as Florence Lane for another quarter mile before rejoining the main road. The original road through this area had many curves traveling over the hilly terrain, although by the 1950s it had been straightened significantly. Another such view of the original alignment is a half-mile further south, where Ransom Road veers to the right (west), rejoining the main road a mile later. The old road is again seen less than a half-mile later, where it travels to the west as a narrow path called Glenwood Lane, curving back across the road shortly thereafter and continuing on the east side for a short distance as Underwood Road and Scales Road before rejoining the main road. The next section is a mile later in Shady Spring, where Marshall Circle turns to the right, rejoining the road a mile later. Shortly thereafter is Lamar Circle, veering east of the road before curving back across and continuing on the west side as Cherry Creek Road, which rejoins the main road a mile later. At Cool Ridge are two more brief segments of the original road, both on the west side of the cur-

Views of The Resort at Glade Springs, covering hundreds of acres east of Route 19/21 between Daniels and Shady Spring [from www.gladesprings.com].

rent one: Madoc Circle and Shilow Circle.

Approximately two miles south of Daniels is the entrance to The Resort at Glade Springs, a year-round world-class resort with three golf courses, a spa, over 200 guest rooms, and many on-site amenities. It operates in conjunction with the Winterplace Ski Resort on Flat Top Mountain, eleven miles south in Ghent. Opened in the mid-1970s, Winter-place has twenty-eight slopes covering nearly 100 acres, with a base elevation around 3,000 feet and a top elevation of 3,600 feet near the peak of Flat Top, and is one of the region's most popular ski resorts.

Continuing south, the road arrives in Shady Spring, a census-designated place with population just over 2,000. Throughout this area, the road maintains a mix of residential and rural surroundings, although the area around Shady Spring has seen increasing growth in recent years with new housing due to its proximity to Beckley, the resorts, and Interstate 77. South of

The West Virginia Turnpike

While Route 21 was the main road from Parkersburg to Charleston to Bluefield in the early 1900s, it was far from an efficient driving experience. Many of those who traveled the road before the interstate era can remember climbing hills in a line of traffic behind slow coal trucks, or getting carsick from the many curves along the way. By the end of World War II, transportation was becoming an increasing priority on a local and national level, and as a result a turnpike commission was established in West Virginia in 1949. Five years later its result was the opening of the 88-mile long turnpike stretching from the east end of Charleston (today Exit 96 of I-77) south to

(right) Northern end of the turnpike at the Kanawha River, with Routes 21/60 running horizontally, parallel to the river.

Creeper Lane Section south of Flat Top through scenic towering stratified shale formation, on the West Virginia Turnpike

U.S. Route 460 near Princeton (today Exit 9 of I-77), traversing some of the state's most treacherous mountain territory. Some original plans for the road had it covering the entire state from Parkersburg to Bluefield, but the current course was ultimately chosen due to budget restrictions. Once opened, the road cut twenty-two miles off of the trip from Charleston to Princeton, but more importantly, with a speed limit of sixty miles per hour compared to the stop-and-go traffic along Route 21, it sped up the trip by nearly two hours. Costing roughly $133 million to build, the road had six exits, three service areas, seventy-six bridges, and one tunnel along its course, and most of the road was just two lanes, one in each direction. Starting at an elevation of 600 feet near Charleston, the road rose an average of forty-three feet per mile to 3,400 feet at Flat Top Mountain, before descending to 2,400 feet at Princeton.

Entrance to Memorial Tunnel on the West Virginia Turnpike

Once the interstate system arrived in the 1960s, the turnpike became part of Interstate 77, with toll-free sections north of the turnpike connecting it to Ohio, and south of the turnpike connecting it to Virginia and the Carolinas. By 1988, the northern portion of the road also carried Interstate 64, from Charleston to just south of Beckley. These connections brought a dramatic increase in traffic to the road, which by the 1970s had become an increasing safety problem. The situation was particularly bad in the mountainous stretches to the south where the two undivided lanes encountered steep hills and sharp curves, and out-of-state drivers were used to four-lane roads with more safety features. As a result, a dramatic improvement project began in the late 1970s, at a final cost of $683 million. Ultimately lasting ten years, the project was completed in 1987, by which time the entire road had been enlarged to four divided lanes, the number of exits had been increased from six to fifteen, and the Memorial Tunnel had been bypassed by a huge cut in the nearby mountain.

Aerial View, showing the Turnpike Roadway, Winding its way through the vicinity of Piney Creek on the West Virginia Turnpike

Today the road is completely at interstate standards and the majority of it has a speed limit of seventy miles per hour. For a standard car, traveling through the three toll booths along its course costs $3.75 (as of 2009). Certainly it is one of the most scenic stretches of interstate highway in the country, and is ideal for anyone traveling through the area in a hurry. Historically, its success was a primary reason that U.S. 21 was decommissioned in the state, although with the turnpike taking the majority of traffic through the area, traveling on Old 21 today is much more enjoyable.

Sand Stone along the West Virginia Turnpike

Shady Spring, the road's local name changes from Ritter Drive to Flat Top Road. Two miles further south is the unincorporated locality of Cool Ridge, and another four miles south brings the road to the similarly unincorporated community of Ghent (mile 354), the second community along Old 21 with that name (the other being in northern Ohio). Running east from the main road here is the entrance to Flat Top Lake, a private community of homes on a man-made lake along Glade Creek, covering 2,200 acres. At the unofficial center of

Ghent is the Ski Barn store, and the intersection with Odd Road, from which Exit 28 of Interstate 77 can be seen less than a half-mile away. Just south of this is the entrance to the previously mentioned Winterplace Ski Resort, after which the main road curves east around the mountain at an elevation of approximately 2,900 feet and through the unincorporated locality of Flat Top.

It was at this remote site that one of the major events in Route 21's history took place, prior to the road officially being marked with signs. Most of what became Route 21 through the region was either part of the old, obsolete Raleigh-Grayson Turnpike or was new construction altogether. Due to the sparse population around Flat Top, this was the last segment of the route in the state to be paved and officially upgraded to the standards of the federal route system. On October 28, 1926, a ceremony took place around the actual paving of the last small section of the road at Flat Top Mountain, similar to the driving of the Golden Spike at Promontory Summit, Utah in 1869, to commemorate the completion of the first transcontinental railroad. Viewing the lengthy motorcade and numerous speeches were an estimated 10,000 people, including many state officials as well as some from Ohio, Virginia, and the Carolinas, as those

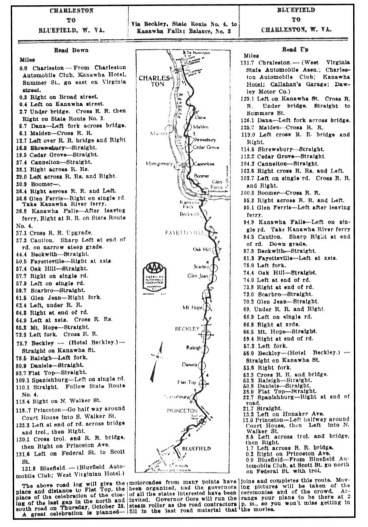

states were to be significantly affected by the improved travel through the mountains. One official from Ohio claimed that the completion of this route cut 286 miles off of the trip from his state to Florida (a number far more significant at that time even than it is today). This was a huge event for residents in the southern part of the state, particularly in Bluefield and Princeton, who had been geographically isolated from the rest of the

---

(above) Simple directions were adequate in guiding motorists along what would soon become U.S. Route 21 when it was completed between Charleston and Bluefield; this appeared in the Bluefield *Daily Telegraph* on October 24, 1926, and still included the ferry at Glen Ferris; **(below)** Local headline for the celebration of the road's completion.

(left) Brochure from Camp Creek State Park; (right) Postcard views of Routes 19/21 between Flat Top Mountain and Princeton in the 1940s; (below left) Actual photographs of the road in 2000.

country but would soon find that changing for the better. It was around this time that the route became known as the "Lakes to Florida Highway," although some local residents pushed for the road to be named as the Shawnee Trail, after the Native American tribe that once populated southern West Virginia (that name never became official). Shortly after the road's completion, approximately 100 of the shield-shaped signs for Routes 19 and 21 were placed along the road from Flat Top to Bluefield, where more roadwork had yet to be completed.

Back in the present, Route 19/21 soon enters Mercer County, the furthest south of the seven counties covered by Route 21 in the state. From this point, the route is known as Beckley Road, curving back west and over the interstate, before running closely parallel to the highway for the next six miles. This section is very sparsely populated with increasingly rocky terrain. The road

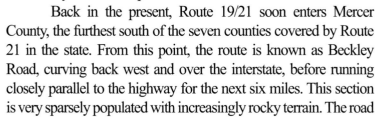

soon crosses over the interstate yet again and through the unmarked locality of Dunns, before gradually descending into a valley to intersect the interstate at Exit 20. This is the first direct inter-

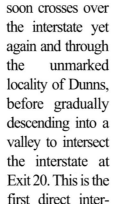

section between I-77 and Old 21 since Exit 96 in Charleston, the northern end of the WV Turnpike, seventy-six miles to the north (see box on page 59).

After passing under the interstate bridge, the road comes to a small unincorporated area known as Camp Creek (mile

(right) Steel arch bridge over the Bluestone River near Spanishburg; built in the 1920s, it is seen here in 1994, but has since been replaced with a modern bridge.

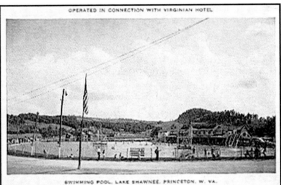

(left) Two postcard views of Shawnee Lake circa 1950; in the top view, the Bluestone River is seen in the foreground; (below) The ferris wheel and portions of other rides are all that remain today [bottom photo taken by Karen Stuebing].

365), so named because it was felt to be a good area for camping by troops during the Civil War. By the 1930s, the area had become one of the major sites for logging by the Blue Jay Lumber Company mentioned earlier. In 1945, the state began to purchase large tracts of land for the purpose of creating the Camp Creek State Forest, which then opened in 1953 with 5,269 acres. In 1987, 550 acres of the forest were set aside to create the Camp Creek State Park for camping, hunting, and fishing. The park's entrance is along Route 19 just south of the interstate, and the creek itself passes under the main road just beyond the park entrance. Continuing south, the terrain becomes more hilly and the road becomes a constant series of curves until the road enters the valley of the Bluestone River, and the unincorporated community of Spanishburg (mile 370). The river has an even more winding course than the road, crossing under the road three times over the next few miles; it travels east from this area to drain into the New River. Continuing south, Old Spanishburg Road runs southeast off of the main route, traveling through a long series of tight curves approximately two miles across a particularly hilly area before rejoining the

main route further south. This was likely part of the Raleigh-Grayson Turnpike through the area, going back to the 1850s, but was not part of the U.S. 19/21 alignment in 1926.

Just past the third crossing of the Bluestone River, the former site of the Shawnee Lake (also known as Lake Shawnee) amusement park can be seen just west of the road. The site has an interesting history going back more than two centuries, when Mitchell Clay established a farm here in 1775 as the first European settler in the area. Local legend states that in 1783, a group of Shawnee Indians attacked Clay's farm while he was away hunting, killing his son and daughter. A second son, Ezekiel, was captured and taken north to the Shawnee city of Chillicothe in the Ohio Territory, where he was burned at the stake. Well into the Twentieth Century, arrowheads and other Native American artifacts could be found at the site, as it had

GREEN LAWN TOURIST CAMP
5 Miles North of Princeton, W. Va.,
on Routes 19 and 21

(left) Century-old building that appears to have been either a church or school in the past, just north of Princeton; (below left) Tourist Camp in the 1940s, near Shawnee Lake.

been part of their territory for generations and the site is thought to have been part of an Indian burial ground. In 1924, Conley Snidow purchased the property and opened Shawnee Lake for swimming, as well as a dance pavilion and later numerous rides. This remained in business until 1966; it reopened nearly twenty years later before closing for good in 1988. While the remains of the rides and some buildings still stand today, the lake is used for local fishing contests and has become legendary as a "haunted" park, due to its history as a graveyard, the murder of the settlers, and various stories (accurate or not) of people that died at the amusement park over the years. It appeared on the television show "The Scariest Places On Earth" in 2005 and has become a popular cult location for those seeking paranormal phenomena.

Continuing on Route 19, the intersection with state Route 10 is immediately south of the former park. One of the longer state highways, this one travels west from this point to Huntington near the Ohio River. Beyond this, the road takes a winding course over more hills and through the unincorporated community of Kegley (mile 376). It then begins to descend toward the county seat of Princeton, at an elevation of 2,450 feet and with a population of more than 6,300; it is part of the Princeton-Bluefield micropolitan area that has more than 107,000 residents in West Virginia and Virginia. Entering the city's north side as Pike Street, the route turns east after several blocks onto Honaker Avenue. Three blocks later it turns south onto North Walker Street, which heads directly for the county courthouse in the city's center (mile 380). The courthouse was built in 1930 to replace an earlier

Bird's-Eye View of Princeton, W. Va. from Route 19 and 21

Mercer County Court House, Princeton, W. Va.

Victorian style building; the current structure is built of an Art Moderne style and is listed on the National Register of Historic Places. It sits in a block between Main and Princeton Streets, where Walker Street splits into two short one-way roads; Scott Street is one-way going south, with Alvis Road being one-way going north. Main Street is also numbered as state Route 20, a

(top right) Birdseye view of Princeton in the 1940s; (above) Mercer County Courthouse in the 1940s; one can faintly see shield-shaped signs for Routes 19, 21, and 219, which ended here at that time and was later replaced in this area by Route 460; the courthouse appears largely the same today; (left) Low-budget Airway Motel on the south side of Princeton in the late 1950s.

SCENE ON ROUTE 21, BETWEEN BLUEFIELD AND PRINCETON, W. VA.

(left) View of the East River Valley from Country Girl Road/Old 21 east of Bluefield; (below right) Small roadside motel in the 1950s.

lengthy road which travels from the Ohio River near New Martinsville to Bluewell, a small town near Bluefield. East of the courthouse, Route 20 follows a portion of Old U.S. Route 460, which has since been rerouted to a main highway nearby.

Beyond the courthouse, Scott and Alvis come together to form South Walker Street, which then continues out of town as Courthouse Road. A little more than a mile beyond the city limits, the road merges with the Big Laurel Highway and U.S. 460, a major east-west route that travels from Norfolk, VA. west to Frankfort, KY., although at one time it continued west to St. Louis. From this point, U.S. 19 travels with 460 southwest for several miles through Green Valley and Stoney Gap, before exiting onto Princeton Avenue on the east side of Bluefield. Meanwhile, the original alignment of what was at the time U.S. 19, 21, and 460 is more challenging to trace. This route traveled several blocks south from the courthouse in Princeton and east onto Old

RAINBOW MOTEL ON US 19, US 21, US 460, BLUEFIELD, W. VA

Bluefield Road, a winding road that parallels the Big Laurel Highway before crossing New Route 19/Courthouse Road and continuing west of that as Green Valley Road. This veers to the south at the unincorporated locality of Glenwood, before continuing as Maple Acres Road/Old U.S. 19 through the localities of Maple Acres and Green Valley. In the latter area, the road intersects state Route 123, which begins here and travels west to the Virginia state line. The key to following Old 21 here is to make a quick jog from Old U.S. 19 left/east onto Route 123, then an immediate right onto

Greetings from Bluefield, W. Va.

Federal Street at Night, Bluefield, W. Va.

(above left) Aerial view of the city in the 1970s; one can see Old 21 ascending East River Mountain in the background; (left) Nighttime view of downtown Bluefield in the 1950s; (above right) Four U.S. highways converged at the intersection of Princeton and Federal Streets in central Bluefield in the 1960s, prior to the construction of the Big Laurel Expressway [Michael Summa collection]; (right) Entering the town heading west along Princeton Avenue in the 1960s; note the large rail yard to the right.

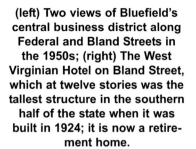

(left) Two views of Bluefield's central business district along Federal and Bland Streets in the 1950s; (right) The West Virginian Hotel on Bland Street, which at twelve stories was the tallest structure in the southern half of the state when it was built in 1924; it is now a retirement home.

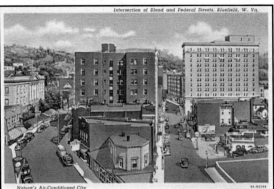

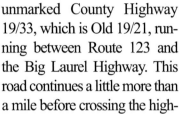

unmarked County Highway 19/33, which is Old 19/21, running between Route 123 and the Big Laurel Highway. This road continues a little more than a mile before crossing the highway and continuing on the south side of it as Country Girl Road for another two miles. Through this stretch it skirts the edge of the East River Valley, dropping from an elevation of 2,800 feet to 2,400 feet, at which point it joins state Route 112, which travels from this point east fourteen miles to Oakvale. The road then continues west, merging shortly thereafter with New Route 19, which is exiting at that point from the Big Laurel Expressway, and the road then continues into Bluefield as Princeton Avenue. The road parallels East River and three sets of railroad tracks immediately to the north through this area. Although not particularly large, the East River is a New River tributary which begins on nearby East River Mountain. An older, winding alignment still exists on the north side of the tracks as Old Princeton Road or Raleigh Grayson Turnpike, connecting from the Big Laurel Expressway on the east end to Princeton Avenue a mile west towards town. The Raleigh-Grayson Turnpike was the earliest version of U.S. 21, traveling from Beckley (which at the time was known as Raleigh Courthouse) to Grayson County in southern Virginia. Built in the mid-1800s, it was an unpaved trail that traversed some very challenging territory from here south through the mountains. Some of it was later bypassed and some was incorporated into the modern road. The name still appears on old roads in several places and is discussed in more detail in the Virginia chapter.

Driving west on Princeton Avenue, the first road on the left is Grassy Branch Road, which carried the Route 21 bypass around downtown beginning in the 1940s. As mentioned previously, U.S. 21 was decommissioned in West Virginia in 1974, although it did still exist from Bluefield south into Virginia until 1980, when it was decommisioned for nearly fifty miles further south to its current northern end in Wytheville. Back on Princeton Avenue, the road soon enters the city of Bluefield, with its population of nearly 11,500. The city, like most of Mercer County and most of the state, developed

(above left) The Bailey Building, at the intersection of Bland and Federal Streets, housed the headquarters of the Appalachian Power Company for years; today it houses a branch of Bluefield State College; (left) One of the early motels along the Route 21 bypass south of the city.

(left) Driving south on Bland Road just south of Bluefield, East River Mountain looms in the distance.

around the coal and railroad industries, with a large rail yard for the Norfolk and Western Company occupying an extensive portion of the downtown area. Depending on the source, the city's name comes from either the presence of large numbers of chicory flowers on the surrounding hillsides, giving the area a bluish color in the summertime, or else from the nearby coal fields surrounding the Bluestone River. One of the state's highest incorporated cities at an elevation of 2,655 feet, it is often referred to as "Nature's Air-Conditioned City."

Old 21 continues on Princeton Avenue until turning south on Bland and Federal Streets, which split the route into two one-way streets through the central business district (Mile 393). At this point, the road leaves Route 19, which continues west on its eventual path to Florida. Old 21, however, is joined at this same point by U.S. Route 52, which originally shared the road with Old 21 from here to Wytheville. Route 52 is a lengthy highway traveling more than 2,000 miles from the Canadian border in North Dakota to the Atlantic Ocean at Charleston, South Carolina. From this point, Federal Street carries traffic north, with Bland Street carrying it south, although after several blocks the roads converge and Bland Street continues south out of the city.

Downtown Bluefield has a more urban appearance than many cities in the region, mainly due to the influx of money from the booming coal and railroad industries in the early part of the 1900s, leading to the building of numerous "skyscrapers" which still stand today. As the road continues south through the locality of South Bluefield, it rejoins the former Route 21 bypass at Cumberland Road.

Returning to Grassy Branch Road on the city's east side, Old 21 was routed south on this road in the 1940s to bypass the busy downtown area. The road covers almost two miles of very rural landscape before ending abruptly on East Cumberland Road in the locality of Cumberland Heights. This is U.S. 52 today, and following Old 21 takes one right (west) for about a mile through one of the area's oldest suburban commercial districts. Being along Route 21 encouraged the growth of numerous motels and restaurants beginning around 1950, and many of them remain open today. At the west end of the commercial district, Cumberland Road intersects Bland Road at a key point along both Routes 21 and 52. Originally, both routes continued west from here on West Cumberland Road (today state Route 598), turning south (left) several blocks later on Washington Street, which curves into Cherry Drive and continues up to the Big Laurel Expressway

View from East River Mountain on Route 21 and 52, Bluefield, W. Va., Nature's Air Conditioned City

(top right) The mountaintop lookout area has been improved greatly in recent years; (right) Two views from the top of East River Mountain; downtown Bluefield is not visible due to a smaller ridge that stands between the mountain and the city.

67

Ridge Runner Railroad

(U.S. 460). Jogging slightly to the west, the old route then continued south as Bland Road and began to ascend the winding path a little more than two miles to the top of East River Mountain and the Virginia state line. In 1980, when U.S. 21 was decommissioned in West Virginia, U.S. 52 was routed away from the mountain, instead traveling east on East Cumberland Road to a junction with the Big Laurel Expressway. It then travels on that road for a little over a mile before following the John F. Nash highway (named for the renowned mathemetician on whose life the film "A Beautiful Mind" was based; he was born and raised in Bluefield) for two miles to a junction with Interstate 77, with both roads then traveling through the East River Mountain Tunnel (which is described in greater detail in the Virginia chapter). If Route 21 had not been decommissioned, it undoubtedly would have been rerouted through the tunnel as well. Once these changes had been made, the old alignment of 21 and 52 up the mountain was renumbered as state Route 598, with the portion on the Virginia side also numbered as state Route 598.

Looking at the original Raleigh-Grayson Turnpike through the area, it more or less followed the course of original Route 21 into Bluefield, then traveled along or near the course of Cumberland Road, approximately three miles east of Route 598, then began to ascend the mountain in an eastbound direction, with many sharp curves along the way. Upon reaching the top at the state line, it cut back to the west and is covered in the Virginia Chapter.

Back on modern Route 598, the tightly winding road ascends nearly 800 feet over its two-mile length, to an elevation of 3487 feet at the peak, where there is a parking lot and picnic facilities to take in the view. This section on the north side of the mountain was completed in late 1927, giving local residents a relatively quick way (52 miles) to access Wytheville. Prior to that, travelers were forced to either take treacherous, narrow, winding local roads over the mountain, or follow a detour far west (143 miles) through Abingdon, VA. to reach Wytheville. Progress of the road's construction and paving were followed on a weekly basis by the Bluefield Daily Telegraph, as its completion was highly anticipated by local residents. During the 1960s and 70s, when all traffic was still forced to travel across the mountain, the Ridge Runner Railroad operated at the top, literally straddling the state line. Consisting of a miniature locomotive and three cars on a narrow-gauge railway, the ride took passengers around a giant oval, split evenly between the two states. A large gift shop stood across the road, the gutted remnants of which still remain today. After the opening of the tunnel below, traffic across the mountain dropped off drastically, and by the early 1980s the ride and gift shop had closed. The Ridge Runner locomotive was saved however, being relocated at that time to Bluefield City Park, where it remains today. While it has not run in years, as of 2009 there was a local movement afoot to renovate the train and put it in motion again at the park. Once past the mountain's peak, the road crosses into Virginia (Mile 398), where its course continues in the following chapter.

(above) Two views of the Ridge Runner in its heyday, circa early 1970s; billed as the shortest interstate railroad in the world, it offered spectacular views of the valley and surrounding area; (right) Souvenir dish from the gift shop across the road.

U.S. Route 21 in Virginia

The entire state of West Virginia was originally part of the state of Virginia, until the latter seceded from the Union to join the Confederate States of America in 1861 at the beginning of the Civil War. With most of the western counties of the state disagreeing with the motion to secede, they began their own movement to secede from Virginia and remain with the United

States. This movement was passed in the state in late 1861, and two years later the new state was admitted to the Union. At that time, the long line drawn to divide the states went across East River Mountain, at the line between Mercer and Bland Counties. Routes 21 and 52 originally crossed the mountain and passed into Virginia and Bland County at the mountain's peak. Today, that road is state Route 598, which immediately begins to descend the south face of the mountain ridge over four miles of sharp curves, before reaching the base at the intersection with Interstate 77, which exits the East River Mountain Tunnel at that point. Also at that point, U.S. Route 52, which in 1980 was routed away from the mountain and through the tunnel, leaves the interstate at Exit 66 to continue on the original road, with state Route 598 ending at that point. The improvements in the section traveling down the south side of the mountain were completed in the summer of 1928, meaning that U.S. 21 ended at the mountain's top for several months, since the road had already been completed on the West Virginia side. Prior to the road's improvements, the route in Virginia was known as state Route 26 (and before that the Raleigh-Grayson Turnpike); Route 26 was then retired three years later. U.S. Route 52 was added to the road from Bluefield to Wytheville

in 1935 when it was extended south. Despite the many curves descending the mountain, this actually represents a newer and more direct road to replace the narrow and even more winding Raleigh-Grayson Turnpike from the 1800s. That road ascended the mountain on the WV side heading east, somewhat to the east of the modern alignment. Upon reaching the top it cut back to

the west and wound its way down to connect with a currently unnamed trail, which then connected to modern Route 598, roughly half way down the mountain. It then continued south along the course of Route 598.

(top left) The first sight upon entering Virginia at the top of East River Mountain is the gutted gift shop for the old Ridge Runner Railroad, which operated from the 1950s through the early 1980s; (above right) View heading southeast down the mountain on the Virginia side; (left) View of the Virginia-side approach to the East River Mountain Tunnel, with the exit to Route 598/Old 21 in the foreground.

(left/below) Entrance and interior of the East River Mountain Tunnel; (bottom left) Stovers Grocery in Rocky Gap, as seen in 1985; the old general store, a traditional sight in Appalachia, had been razed and replaced with a small modern building within a few years, although the smaller building on the right still stands as of 2009; a gas station still operates at the site today.

The opening of the 5,412-foot East River Mountain Tunnel in December 1974 was a milestone in local transportation, eliminating the requirement to cross the mountain when traveling north and south. With groundbreaking in August 1969, more than five years and $40 million was spent on its construction, although since the state line crosses the tunnel almost exactly at its center, the two states split the bill nearly evenly. The seventh-longest twin-highway tunnel in the country, it is maintained regularly and has provided safe service for more than thirty-five years. The tunnel's construction was welcomed by many local residents, partly for the jobs that it provided for several years, but also for making travel in the area far easier. The following quote is from Bradely Payne, a resident of Rocky Gap, from the Bland County History Archives web site:

"Living in Rocky Gap, VA, you had to travel over East River Mountain to get to Bluefield or Princeton or wherever you was going. Road conditions was very bad. The road were not wide enough in some places for cars to pass each other. There was no guard rails up. The mountain was always foggy at night and in the winter time, very dangerous and treacherous. Well, we did most of our shopping in Bluefield. So in the average, two to three times a week we had to travel from Rocky Gap to Bluefield. Once you got up on the mountain the scenery was beautiful. You could look back on Rocky Gap and you could see the mountains and the valleys, or right on top of East River Mountain you should see the whole town of Bluefield. But the main attraction on East River Mountain, before the tunnel was put in, was the craft shop up there and the train rides. Very nice on East River Mountain, that was the good points. And I'm not mistaken even the tunnel was very good for both sides of the mountain. We lost our attraction up there because there was no traffic then going over East River Mountain, everything was converted through the tunnel. Oh my yes, it's a great improvement. I would give all the luxury of the East River Mountain scenery just to have a safer way backward and forth over the mountain."

Beyond the tunnel, Route 52/Old 21 is known (appropriately enough) as North Scenic Highway and it continues south through the locality of North Gap and into the unincorporated village of Rocky Gap (Mile 404), originally settled in 1763 and having a population today of 78. Despite the mountainous terrain surrounding the village, its elevation is 2,334 feet, which is actually several hundred feet lower than Bluefield on the other side of East River Mountain. The mountains and rocky soil make farming in the area challenging, and as a result the entire county

is sparsely populated, with less than 7,000 residents. In Rocky Gap, the road intersects state Route 61, which travels from Tazewell to Narrows in western Virginia. Original Routes 21/52 continued south at this point, but since the construction of I-77, the road turns briefly west on Route 61 to cross under the interstate at Exit 64 before turning south again on the west side of it. From

Two century-old buildings standing in Rocky Gap in 2001; both remain standing as of 2010

here, Route 52 runs immediately parallel to the interstate for two miles through a narrow gap between Wolf Creek Mountain to the east and Rich Mountain to the west, before turning west through the localities of South Gap and Hicksville.

Prior to the interstate, the road ran along the east bank of Wolf Creek which flows south through this stretch, although the creek now runs between the northbound and southbound lanes of the interstate from here to Rocky Gap. Wolf Creek is a small tributary of the Holsten River, part of the Tennessee River watershed, and is the first body of water along Old 21 since leaving Northeast Ohio that is not part of the Ohio River watershed. Based on old maps, it appears that the northbound lane of I-77 runs through the original alignment of the U.S. highway, and current Route 52 is a newer road built at the time of the interstate's construction. Beyond South Gap, Route 52 crosses Wolf Creek three times over the next few miles on its way to the unincorporated village of Bastian (Mile 412) and the locality of Suiter. From Rocky Gap to this point, the road follows the original right-of-way for the New River, Holsten, and Western Railroad Company that operated to service the local lumber and mining industries between 1914 and 1946. A bit more history of the road comes from an 1990s interview between local resident Jasper Walker, who was born in Bastian in 1914, and Rocky Gap High School student Amy Kitts (from the Bland County History Archives web site):

"They had the first highway to come through Bland Co. was the Raleigh Grayson Turnpike. There was about room for two horses to walk side by side. That's all it was. It went from Grayson County, Virginia to Raleigh County, West Virginia, across East River Mountain, on into Raleigh Co. where Beckley is now. And it was called Highway 21. When they brought the convicts in here and built a highway, they built it by hand power, and named it U.S. 21. And it was a dirt road to start with. And they'd pave it a little every year, and built these bridges, these cement bridges. They was built in 19 and 29. I stood out and watched them work on them bridges." [Newspaper accounts indicate that a total of seven bridges were built to replace previously existing fords across streams, and that indeed, chain gangs of convicts were used as the primary labor force. The bridges, however, were built in 1927, after which the road was up to federal standards and officially became U.S. 21. Additional improvements to various sections of the road were made over the next two years.]

A few other highlights of the interview:

Amy: Were there many cars here when you were a little boy?
Mr. Walker: No.
Mrs. Walker: People were poor all together.
Mr. Walker: One, one car.
Amy: Who had that car?
Mr. Walker: Ah, Doctor Walker. Doctor Walker had a car that he rode in the summer time when the road was good. When it got bad, he rode a horse, Old Bob.
Amy: Was there anything fun to do?
Mr. Walker: Run, run up and down the road and throw rocks at each other.
Amy: What did you do on Christmas?
Mr. Walker: Ah, eat and run around in the snow and get your feet wet.

(right) Route 52/Old 21 running parallel to I-77 just south of Rocky Gap, through the mountain gap;
(above right) Mileage marker in the same area;

Amy: What kind of presents did you get?

Mr. Walker: Not much of any. Ah, little bag of candy, and an orange, and that was about it.

Amy: What did you do on Halloween?

Mr. Walker: Turned the toilets over up and down the road, and up at the school house at Bastian. Turned the toilets over and piled rocks on the porch and throwed a rock or two through windows, and just anything that's mean.

Just before reaching Bastian is the Wolf Creek Indian Village and Museum, a recreation of a Native American village from approximately 800 years ago. Standing at a site where Native American relics have been found, the facility also has nature trails and a picnic area. Beyond Bastian, the road turns back to the southeast toward I-77, to which it runs parallel for the next mile. Beginning somewhat below the level of the interstate, the road rises rapidly, soon finding itself well above the freeway as it climbs the ridge known as Brushy Mountain (I-77 travels through a large cut in the mountain). Soon encountering a sharp hairpin turn, the road soon comes to the top of the ridge at an elevation of 2,826 feet (although the highest point on Brushy Mountain is over 3,100 feet). This elevation along Old 21 was well marked in previous years, although it no longer is. Although not well-marked at this point, the road then crosses the Appalachian Trail, a nearly 2,200-mile hiking trail, established in the 1920s, that extends from Georgia to Maine. The route up Brushy Mountain was rebuilt at the time of the inter-state's construc-

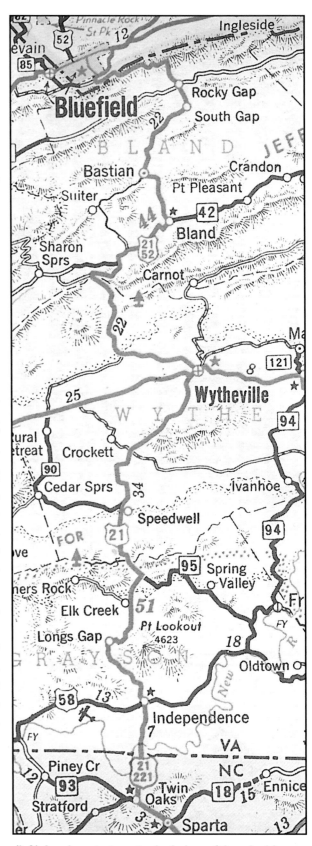

(left) An almost stereotypical view of Appalachia as seen from Routes 21/52 near Bastian; (above left) Church near Bastian; (above) 1949 Esso Gasoline map of U.S. Route 21 in Virginia; the map looks somewhat different today with I-77 running through the region.

(left) Hairpin turn near the top of Brushy Mountain; (bottom left) Early postcard views of the town of Bland, and the 1950s-era Old Dominion motor court; the motor court still stands at the northwest corner of Main Street and South Scenic Highway, in the center of the town; a 1940s-era former gas station with characteristic pillars stands in front of the motel.

tion; the original route traveled north of the current one along state Route 648. This ends at the interstate, but originally continued up the mountain on a winding path north of I-77 that can be seen in aerial views and is faintly visible from the interstate. It then crossed back over where the large cut was made in the mountain for the interstate's construction, and after that it connected to current Route 52 near the hairpin turn. Once at the top of the ridge, the road descends the south side much more gradually. This entire area is part of the Jefferson National Forest, established in 1936 and lying in three states but mostly in Virginia, with a total size of over 700,000 acres. In 1995 it was combined with the George Washington National Forest, the pair covering over 1.8 million acres. As such, this territory is sparsely populated and the road is surrounded primarily by dense woodlands.

After another mile, the road travels under the interstate before continuing south into the town of Bland (Mile 417), which despite being the county seat is unincorporated. The town and county are named for Richard Bland, a revolutionary war hero; the scenery here is anything but bland however, sitting between Brushy and Big Walker Mountains, both of which are visible throughout the area. Entering the town as Main Street, Old 21 intersects state Route 42 coming from the east, where it begins in Woodstock in northern Virginia; it travels west to Broadford in the far-western part of the state. It then encounters Route 98, a peculiar state highway that runs for a mere half-mile within the town of Bland before ending. However, Route 21's predecessor, state Route 26, followed the original Raleigh-Grayson Turnpike along Route 98 to the south end

of town before following what is today secondary state Route 656 and then Forest Service Road 206 over Big Walker Mountain with switchbacks and many tight curves, making it a very difficult ride to the village of Carnot, along modern state Route 717. The road is still denoted by a sign stating "Raleigh Grayson Turnpike" at its intersection with Main Street in Bland. A great description of the old mountain road comes from local resident Jerry Fuhrman in his "From On High" blog on the internet from 2004:

"Raleigh Grayson Turnpike, the road that leads to my place, was carved out of the local landscape in the 1840's. It snakes around my property and works its way up the mountain, across the ridge, and, twelve miles later, down again. An old fella in the area once told me that when he was a child (he's in his 80's), the turnpike was the only route from the village of Bland to the near-

Old Dominion Court & Grill
On U. S. Routes 21 and 52
Bland, Va.

(left) Bland County logo and courthouse on Main Street; this was along the Raleigh-Grayson Turnpike but not U.S. 21; (below) Original twelve-mile section of the Raleigh-Grayson Turnpike over Big Walker Mountain between Bland and Carnot, near Wytheville; most of it still exists today as a trail, but having never been paved, it is very difficult to follow [map courtesy of John Dodson at the Bland County History Archives].

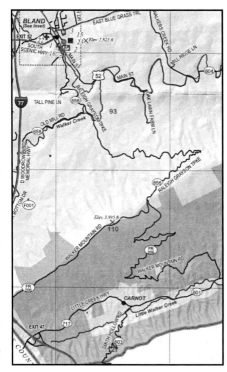

est town, Wytheville. He told me about the special day-long journeys his family would make over the mountain in the mule-drawn wagon in order to buy supplies. I've traveled this route. In places, high up on the mountain, the passage narrows. It is sometimes so narrow that if you stray off the road at all, you're faced with a precipitate drop of hundreds of feet. I get a little nervous riding this road on my ATV. They made this trek in the old days in a mule drawn wagon.

I'm told the turnpike was built with slave labor. And oxen were used for the heavy lifting. There is evidence readily seen, all along the route, of boulders that were cleared from the roadbed and dragged to the side. Massive boulders. How the slaves must have worked at it. How many years it must have taken them. The road was still in use until 1972 when the state of Virginia opened up the last section of I-77. The last section involved a tunnel cut right through Big Walker Mountain, my mountain. When I-77 was completed, the state of Virginia abandoned that portion of the old Raleigh Grayson Turnpike that runs from my property to the mountaintop and along the ridge. It's still there. But it hasn't been upgraded in years. It is as it was. The roadbed is in poor condition. It's probably not much worse than it was a century ago but it's still a rugged ride for someone with a weak stomach. It was never paved. Truth be known, much of it is dirt. The more luxurious stretches contain a layer of rocks, most of which are the size of a dinner plate. The only vehicle traffic on the pike now involves the occasional logging truck and lots of hunters on all-terrain vehicles

It is here on the pike that the Old South comes alive. A walk up the mountain is a journey into the past. On any given day, if you keep an eye out while you labor up the old trail, you can find treasure lying in the roadway. This spring Paula and I were walking back from a hike up the mountain when suddenly she noticed, half buried in the dirt, an old horseshoe. Paula pulled it out of the road and immediately noticed that it was too big to have come from a horse (most folks here in the mountains didn't own large draft horses; Belgians and the like required too much forage in an area where grazing land was at a premium). It had to be a mule shoe. One's imagination runs to thoughts of Colonel Toland's Yankee raid that came up the pike in 1864. It could have come off of one of their pack mules. It's also possible that it simply came from a mule belonging to one of the local residents a long, long time ago. We put the mule shoe back where we found it. It is again making history.

(right) Postcard and real views of the approach to Big Walker Mountain from the north along modern Routes 21/52.

(left) Abandoned Shell gas station near the north base of Big Walker Mountain along modern Route 52, as seen in 1994; the building still stands as of 2009 but the gas pumps, having become prized collectibles, are long gone; (below left) A throwback to the 1950s and before that, shield-shaped route signs remained in service in western Virginia well into the 1990s [photo courtesy of Michael Summa]; (below right) Another view looking up at Big Walker Mountain from Routes 21/52.

We have found plenty of other treasure along the turnpike. Included in our cache are pieces of harness, lots of pottery shards, pieces of plates and cups (some with beautiful design patterns), a belt buckle, and a few shotgun shells from more recent times. The area where many of the artifacts can be found is right at the base of the mountain, which would lead one to believe that the remains are some of the loot confiscated from local villagers by Yankee marauders 160 years ago and discarded - in an effort to shed heavy baggage - when the soldiers involved saw the climb they were about to face. We haven't come upon any gold coins yet but I keep looking.

The best part of the story is that it will always be as it is, as it was. I'd invite you to take a journey into history with us but first I have a warning. Be careful. There is a saying that I heard a number of years ago. If you come to our tiny corner of the Old South to walk the Raleigh Grayson Turnpike, "take but a picture; leave but a footprint."

From Carnot, the original road continued south on modern state Route 603/Smith Hollow Road, another difficult, twisting road over Little Walker Mountain. It then followed Cove Road into Wytheville, where it followed Peppers Ferry Road, East Monroe Street, North 11th Street, and finally East Main Street to meet up with modern Route 21. While some sources suggest that Route 21 briefly followed the old turnpike in the 1920s before being routed west along its later alignment, the turnpike was actually in use as state Route 26 only until 1926, when Route 21 was being established. At that time it was rerouted, so the new U.S. highway never followed the original turnpike (which was not up to the standards of the federal road

(left) One of many scenic views from the top of Big Walker Mountain, with its rhododendrons in bloom; (above right) Generic postcard from the top.

75

(left) Entrance to the Big Walker Mountain Tunnel; (below left) Aerial View of the same, showing the size of the mountain and the extent of wilderness on its slope; (below right) The top of the mountain in 2001; the elevation at the site is actually 3,405 feet, and the 3,787 elevation refers to the ridge's peak nearby.

system) over the mountain [Thanks to Michael Roberson of www.vahighways.com for his extensive research on this subject].

Historically, the Raleigh-Grayson turnpike was a monumental undertaking for its time, considering the topography of the region. The Upper New River Valley in southwestern Virginia and western North Carolina was largely isolated from the remainder of both states and was difficult to reach even into the mid-1800s. The turnpike was built between the late 1840s and approximately 1860, and covered more than 150 miles from Beckley (aka Raleigh Courthouse) through Princeton, Bluefield, Wytheville, and through the Elk Creek Valley to Independence and the North Carolina line. The Grayson County portion was approximately 20

Observation Tower Atop Big Walker Mountain

From this Tower at Big Walker Lookout, 5 States can be Viewed

miles in length and cost, at the time, the sum of $425 per mile, or nearly $9,000. The specifications for the road were sixteen feet in width, macadamized ditches along each side, and to have all trees, rocks and stumps removed from the road path, a revolution in mountain road-building. The Raleigh-Grayson turnpike was not paved, however, and during the rainy, snowy winters and springs of Appalachia, the road became nearly impassible due to mud. Sharp, narrow wagon tires wore deep ruts in the road, and constant repair was needed to keep the road intact. Despite its faults, the Raleigh-Grayson Turnpike became the key

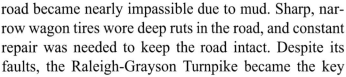

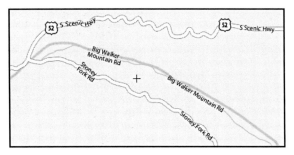

(above left) Original fifty-foot lookout tower built by Stuart Kime in the early 1950s; within several years it had doubled in height; (left) Local map of Old 21/Route 52 today as it climbs Big Walker Mountain; the grey line is the Bland/ Wythe County line and represents the top of the ridge that makes up the mountain; (above right) Historical markers on the southbound side of the road, indicating that Wythe County was named after George Wythe, a signer of the Declaration of Independence, and giving information about Toland's Raid.

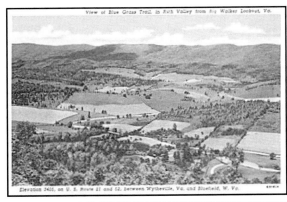

View of Blue Grass Trail in Rich Valley from Big Walker Lookout, Va.

Elevation 3461, on U. S. Route 21 and 12, between Wytheville, Va. and Bluefield, W. Va.

(left) Postcard view of the valley below Big Walker Lookout; (below left) Three actual views in different directions; on a clear day it was said that parts of five states could be seen from this point, but frequently the mist can make it hard to even see the nearby valley; (below right) Two views of the lookout at its peak in the 1960s.

Big Walker Lookout

route in and out of the New River Valley from the 1850s through the early part of the Twentieth Century. This was the route along which Grayson County's soldiers marched off to war, and it had strategic value for fighting in the region, with several small skirmishes taking place along its course. This was also the road on which Upper New River products were shipped out and the way that news of the outside world came in, as there was no telegraph office anywhere in the Upper New River Valley until well after the Civil War ended. (This information edited from www.newrivernotes.com, an excellent source of history from the region.)

Back in Bland, modern Route 52/Old 21 was opened in 1926 as an alternative to the turnpike; it turns west with Route 42 onto what is now called South Scenic Highway in the center of town. The road then travels less than a mile before crossing I-77 at Exit 52; the next sixteen miles going south are labeled as the Big Walker Mountain National Scenic Byway. The road then continues southwest past the Big Walker Motel; four miles later Routes 52 and 42 split near the locality of Effna. Route 52 continues south and then west as it heads toward Big Walker Mountain. Although this stretch of highway has retained its U.S. highway status, it lost most of its traffic upon the opening of the Big Walker Mountain Tunnel along the interstate in 1972. At 4,229 feet in length, the tunnel took five years to build, costing approximately $50 million and cutting the drive time from Bland County to Wytheville by 30 minutes. It also gives Bland

(left) Lookout in the 1960s, when the ski lift was still in operation, taking visitors over the road to a higher spot on the ridge for picnics, viewing, etc.; (below left) The swing bridge connected the gift shop to the tower and is still in place today; (bottom left) Aerial view of the lookout site, showing the dramatic landscape to the southwest, including the peak of Griffith Knob, which is roughly the same height as Big Walker Mountain.

County the distinction of being the nation's only county requiring passage through a tunnel to both enter and exit the county.

The trip over Big Walker Mountain requires such a drive to the west and back to the east that it appears as a noticeable notch on statewide maps. The two miles of tight hairpin curves on each side of the mountain provide the most challenging driving along the entire length of Old 21. However, the views from the top are worth the drive, which can make even the hardiest passengers carsick. Once reaching the top (Mile 426), one reaches the approximate half-way point along the original length of Old 21. The peak of Big Walker Mountain is officially listed at 3,787 feet in elevation, referring to the high point along the ridge nearby, although a similar sign posted in 1985 had it listed as 3,405 feet, which is the elevation where the road crosses. Either way it is the high point along the entire length of Old 21, as well as being the official line between Bland and Wythe Counties.

Through the years it has also been one of the most tourist-oriented sites along the entire course of old Route 21, with the Big Walker Lookout operating at the site since 1947. Stuart Kime was an aircraft engineer from Pennsylvania who founded the lookout after working at a mountaintop tourist stop in the Ozark Mountains and deciding that he wanted to run a similar business himself. In 1945 he purchased a small tavern atop Big Walker, along with thirty-five surrounding acres of land. Two years later he had converted the bar into a gift shop and gas station, and in the coming years he added a full-service restaurant, known as the Pioneer Dining Room, and a fifty-foot observation tower, which he built himself. He later hired a company to rebuild this as a 100-foot tower with an adjacent swinging bridge, and a chair lift over the road to a higher elevation where there was a picnic area and a replica of an old moonshine cabin. For a number of years, there was also a snake pit in an area under the tower. Eventually the restaurant and store filled 4,000

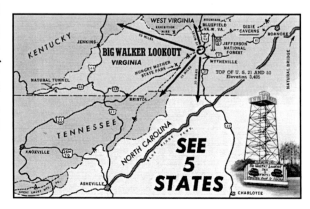

Early 1950s postcard showing the five states visible from the lookout; today only three states are generally visible.

(right) View of the lookout store in 1968, still during the boom years; (below) View of the tower from the far side of the swing bridge and from its base.

square feet, and in the lower level was a 4,000 square foot area for the family home and an adjacent 2,500 square foot workshop. Kime designed and built the new structure himself. The interior of the building had paneling of wormy chestnut, and the open ceiling beams were all more than 250 years old.

The lookout has remained a family business ever since; Stuart kept the books while his wife Abigail was the restaurant manager. In addition, she was also the pastry chef and became famous for her homemade pies and cupcakes. Her

banana cream and coconut cream pies and devil's food cupcakes with chocolate mocha icing were customer favorites. The lookout and restaurant were open year-round, and during the busiest times, Abigail made up to thirty pies each day. On Sundays, not just tourists but many local residents came to the restaurant for pan-fried chicken dinners with all of the trimmings for $1.25. Also, Stuart cured up to 30,000 pounds of ham per year, selling it in the restaurant and around the country. Local sheriff's deputies had to direct traffic at the mountain site on the busiest days when the parking lot was overflowing along the busy highway. Seemingly everyone who traveled the road stopped at the lookout, and even Guy Lombardo

and his orchestra once stopped there to eat.

Despite Kime's success with the lookout, he continued to look for new things to add to the site. By the early 1960s, when he had run out of additional parking space for patrons, he opened a second site at the south base of the mountain. Originally intended to provide additional parking with a train that would bring customers to the lookout at the top, it eventually evolved into the Dry Gulch

SCENIC VIEWS
Big Walker Lookout
OBSERVATION TOWER
SWINGING BRIDGE
ELEVATION 3405
HIKING TRAILS
OVERLOOK of the BIG WALKER NATIONAL SCENIC BYWAY
CRAFT SHOP
GIFTS - SOUVENIRS
LUNCH SHOP

(left) Two views of the lookout store in 2001, two years before the fire; the building was definitely showing its age by this time and a handful of cars was typical instead of a full parking lot; (above right) Modern advertisement for the lookout.

(right) View looking down through the tower; (below right) Inside the original gift shop [photo taken by Kevin Wise]; (bottom right) View of the road at the county line from the top of the tower and the gift shop as seen from the top; the building was much larger than it appeared from the road, and it had two floors of living space for the owners below the gift shop.

Junction Theme Park. With a train ride to take customers throughout the property, staged gun battles between heroes and villains, and recreations of various "old west" type buildings such as a saloon, hotel, and mortuary, the site had the feel of a western movie set.

By this time, it had become clear that the state was considering building a new interstate highway nearby to bypass the old road. Although Kime knew this would cause a dramatic drop in business, he was supportive of the construction of I-77 because having the interstate nearby was preferable to having it built some distance away, which would leave the area isolated and likely kill his business altogether. The arrival of the interstate was another reason that he built Dry Gulch Junction, figuring that two attractions were more likely to draw travelers off the interstate and up the mountain than just one.

As fate would have it, Kime died in 1972, the same year the interstate opened. Abigail, however, kept the lookout going as a seasonal operation from April to October until she retired in 1991. Their son Ron took it over the following year and his son Michael joined the business in later years. The lookout endured some tough times after the interstate opened and business dropped off as predicted. The full restaurant had closed in 1965, although the dining room remained in place as a snack bar. The snake pit was later removed and the chair lift ceased operation in

(left) Two views of the interior of the restaurant in the 1960s when it was still in operation.

(left) Souvenir dish from the gift shop; (right) Charred remains of the building after the fire, as seen six months later in August 2003; (below right) The Kime family quickly built a new gift shop, naming it as the BW Country Store; the swing bridge remains standing in the foreground.

the 1970s. Dry Gulch Junction closed in 1980, although the site reopened on a limited basis as the Virginia City gem mine in 1999, operating for several more years before closing in 2008. Despite this, the lookout remained in business and even began to see a gradual increase in business after this section of U.S. 52 was declared a National Scenic Byway in 1992.

As business continued to grow over the following decade, disaster struck in February 2003 when a fire broke out, destroying the building housing the gift shop, restaurant, and the Kime's home. Due to the remote location, by the time the fire was noted by a passing car and the area fire department came, it was too late to save the building. Fortunately, the tower and swing bridge were not affected by the blaze, and a new gift

shop was built soon afterwards. The site has since returned to being open year-round, with souvenirs and local crafts available for purchase. After more than sixty years, the Kime family continues to operate the site, with Ron working along side his wife, sister, and son. They also operate a large antique mall several miles south along I-77 and 81. Abigail Kime died in 2007.

Today, one can still climb the tower for the price of $5.00. The climb is somewhat harrowing, as the tower shakes noticeably with every step, although the structure is inspected regularly for safety. Upon reaching the top, the view is spectacular at any time of the year, with the mountains of southern West Virginia

(left) Views of the Dry Gulch Junction train ride during the early 1970s; (above right) Lookout site from the road today; as late as the early 2000s, the ski lift pavilion and net that stretched out over the road were still in place although not functional. The tower and new gift shop are all that remain today.

81

Dry Gulch Junction Railroad

visible to the north, Mount Rogers and Whitetop Mountain visible to the southwest, and North Carolina visible in the south. At one time, Tennessee and Kentucky were thought to be visible as well, but haze and air pollution prevent that today.

The lookout's future looks positive today as travelers continue to seek out alternatives to interstate driving, since few points on I-77 afford one the same degree of scenery. This site is at the northern edge of the Blue Ridge Highlands, which extend into North Carolina and Tennessee and are part of the greater Blue Ridge Mountain portion (extending from Georgia to Pennsylvania) of the Appalachian range. This region

Dry Gulch Junction Ghost Town

is so named due to the bluish haze often seen over the mountains, caused by the release of the organic compound isoprene from the millions of trees that line the slopes.

At the Bland/Wythe County line in front of the lookout, the road's name changes to Stony Fork Road, which continues south into Wytheville. Immediately past the lookout is a state historical marker describing

Dry Gulch Junction Saloon

Toland's Raid. The original marker stated *"Over this pass, Union cavalry under Colonel John T. Toland raided to Wytheville to destroy the Virginia and Tennessee Railway (N & W), July 1863. Mary Tynes, a girl of the neighborhood, rode ahead to warn the people. When the raiders reached Wytheville, they were repulsed by home guards and Toland was killed."* That marker

has been replaced with new wording, as follows: *"Col. John T. Toland of the 34th Regiment Mounted Ohio Volunteer Infantry, leading Federal Cavalrymen, marched from Tazewell County and raided Wytheville during the evening of 18 July 1863.*

(left/above) By 1980, Dry Gulch had closed and remained so until 1999 when the site reopened on a much more limited basis as the Virginia City exhibition gem mine.

82

(right) Three miles south of Big Walker Lookout but still in the mountain's shadow, the Deer Trail Park campground sits 1/4 mile off Routes 21/52 on state Route 686; (below left) The first signs of modern Route 21 appear just south of I-81, north of Wytheville; (below right) The Spring Court Motel was advertised as being on Routes 11, 52, and 21, but it was actually on a portion of Main Street shared by Routes 11 and 52, somewhat east of the path of Route 21; (bottom left) Postcard view of Main Street in the 1940s.

Confederate troops under Maj. Thomas M. Bowyer and local citizens fortified in buildings at first withstood the attack, killing Toland. After the Confederates withdrew, federal forces burned several buildings. After learning that Confederate troops were situated at present day Rural Retreat, the federals left Wytheville early the next morning initially headed north towards Walker Mountain." While there is minimal documentation of the events and much of the information is legend or word-of-mouth, it is known that Toland had

a force of nearly 1,000 soldiers, whose goal was to destroy a railroad bridge to disrupt Confederate supply lines, and possibly to also destroy telegraph lines and damage nearby salt and lead mines. The residents of Wytheville were forewarned, and a group of fifty men and boys were able to fight off the Union invaders, shooting Toland through the heart and killing him instantly. It does appear that 26-year-old Mary Elizabeth "Molly" Tynes was the one who warned the residents, having ridden her horse "Fashion" overnight, approximately forty miles from Tazewell over Big Walker Mountain and into Wytheville. It's definitely a story right out of Hollywood.

At the same point as the historical marker, a dirt road goes off to the left. Not well-marked, this is Forest Service Road 206, also known as Big Walker Mountain Road, traveling along the top of the entire ridge. Four miles along that road is the Big Bend picnic area, near a forest service fire tower. The road then continues, eventually connecting to the old Raleigh-Grayson Turnpike

trail previously mentioned. Route 21/52 then begins a two-mile descent over more winding curves before the mountain is just a large dark spot in the rear-view mirror. At the mountain's south base is the site of the former Dry Gulch Junction previously mentioned. Less than a mile

further south, the road insects state Route 717, which carries the Scenic Byway back to I-77, where it ends. Stony Fork Road then continues over a winding and hilly stretch over Little Walker Mountain and then through the unincorporated locality of Favonia before reaching the town limits of Wytheville, where it becomes North 4th Street.

Wytheville, with its population of just over 7,800, is the Wythe County seat. In the early days

(right) South of Wytheville, distance signs are a common site; (below left) View looking south along Route 21 south of Wytheville; the road travels among ridges between 2,200 and 2,800 feet in elevation; (below right) Motel Blackrock was located two miles north of Independence, VA. in the 1940s; the building was still standing as of 2008.

of U.S. 21, the city (roughly at the route's midpoint) was the headquarters for the Lakes-to-Florida Association, later the U.S. 21 Association, which was involved with promoting commerce along the route, and was also instrumental in securing the course of the new Interstate 77, closely following the old U.S. highway's path. On the city's northwest side, North 4th Street crosses Interstate 81 at Exit 70. Interstate 81 travels over 800 miles through the Appalachian Mountains, from the Canadian border with New York to Dandridge, Tennessee. At this junction, U.S. 52 enters the interstate to travel along its course for approximately ten miles east, before exiting to continue on its way south. Also at this junction, we finally see the appearance of U.S. Route 21, which now begins here and heads south through the town. The section from here north to Bluefield lost its numerical designation in 1980. The road then continues a mile into town, where it intersects U.S. Route 11 at West Main Street (Mile 440). U.S. 11 is another lengthy route that runs par-

allel to I-81, traveling over 1,600 miles from the Canadian border with New York to New Orleans, LA. At this point, Route 21 turns right (southwest), sharing the road with Route 11 for four blocks before 11 turns right on North 12th Street/West Lee Highway to head west out of town. Route 21 then continues southwest on West Main for another six blocks before curving to the left (south), at which point it is named as Grayson Road and quickly leaves the downtown area. Looking at the route's original alignment through town, it followed Tazewell Street (which now turns to the left just past the junction with I-81) to Main Street; it was moved to its current alignment on 4th Street in

the mid-1950s. On the south side of town, the road originally turned south off of West Main Street onto South 18th Street, crossing railroad tracks and then turning west onto Railroad Avenue before turning south onto Grayson Road several blocks later. This alignment was abandoned in favor of the current one in 1937 (again, thanks to Michael Roberson for his research on this).

Crossing Fox Creek (a tributary of the New River) a mile or so further south, the road leaves Wytheville altogether, south of which it is known as Grayson Turnpike, as portions of it follow the original Raleigh-Grayson Turnpike from here to Grayson County and eventually the state border with North Carolina. Two segments of the original turnpike are seen as state Route 684; the first segment is known as Winding Road and trav-

els to the west of the modern road for a mile before reconnecting to it. The next segment begins just south of that and is known variously as Stroup Mountain Road, Old Mountain Road, and Chaney Branch Road. It passes considerably to the east of the modern road and follows a very winding path over the hills, with many tight curves. It travels through the locality of Rowe Crossroads before reconnecting with the modern road approximately six miles south of its origin. Throughout this area, the road travels through a valley surrounded by hills that range from 2200 to 2800 feet in elevation. One mile further south, the road crosses Cripple Creek and passes through the unincorporated community of Speedwell (Mile 452). In this area, another part of the original alignment of the turnpike can be seen as Old Bank Road, a quarter-mile to the east, which then crosses the road and continues for a brief stretch on the west side of the road as the unpaved Cave Hill Lane. At Speedwell, the road enters the Mount Rogers National Recreation

Area, an area of over 150,000 acres that was established in 1966 and is under the management of the George Washington and Jefferson National Forests. It is named for Mount Rogers, the state's highest peak at 5,729 feet, which at its nearest point stands approximately twenty miles west of Route 21. Four miles beyond Speedwell, the road enters Grayson County, the last of the three counties the road passes through in Virginia, and the road becomes known as Elk Creek Parkway.

Another two miles south, the road crosses a ridge and descends into the valley of Elk Creek as it leaves the Mount Rogers N.R.A. at the locality of Turkey Fork; shortly thereafter it passes through the unincorporated communities of Elk Creek (Mile 460) and Lower Elk Creek. The next nine miles continue to be very rural and scenic, passing through the locality of Long Gap at one point, with numerous curves and hills. Just to the east is Point Lookout Mountain, which has a peak of 4,600 feet and a portion of which is being developed into homesites. Route 21 then approaches the county seat of Independence with its population of just under 1,000, at which point it is renamed as North Independence Avenue. In the center of town (Mile 469), at the northeast corner of Independence and Main Streets, is the old ornate county courthouse, built in 1908 and in use until 1981 when it was replaced by a modern structure. Today it is used as the Art and Cultural Center of Grayson County and is on the National

(top left) Aerial view of Independence, looking west; (above) Grayson County Courthouse, in use from 1908 to 1981, at the center of town; (left) Multiple route signs at the center of Independence as seen in the late 1980s; Virginia was one of the last states to eliminate the smaller shield-shaped route signs in favor of the larger square signs that are in use today [Michael Summa collection].

(right) Original Doughton Bridge over the New River, just north of the state line; it has since been replaced; (below) View of the river from the New River Campground at the state line

Register of Historic Places. Also at the same intersection, Route 21 intersects U.S. 58, which travels more than 500 miles through southern Virginia, from the ocean at Virginia Beach to the Cumberland Gap area at the border of Virginia and Tennessee. It also joins U.S. Route 221, which is considered a spur of Route 21, traveling more than 700 miles from Lynchburg, VA. to Perry, FL. The two routes share the road south for the next seven miles into North Carolina. There are three other spurs of Route 21 which cross the road in the Carolinas; between 1926 and 1934 there was also a U.S. Route 121, which traveled from near Wytheville to Lexington, NC, but this was later replaced by a rerouted U.S. Route 52. The 121 number will soon return, however, as a new highway through coal country, connecting Beckley, WV and Pound, VA.

After crossing Main Street, Route 21 is known for several blocks as South Independence Avenue, before being renamed as New River Parkway, which it retains to the state line. The road rapidly returns to a sparsely populated rural setting before reaching a second crossing of the New River three miles further south. The original three-arch Doughton Bridge over the river was built around 1928, soon after Route 21 was established, when its paving through the area was fairly primitive. This bridge was replaced by a simple, modern span in the 1990s. The river then runs parallel to the road, immediately to the east of which is the New River Campground (the second establishment with that name along Old 21, the other being in Gauley Bridge, WV). At an eleva-

tion of roughly 2,500 feet, the campground offers canoeing and kayaking, and has overnight cabins, a playground, and picnic facilities. Its position straddles the state line, with the entrance on the Virginia side, although the site maintains an address and phone number in each state. While passing the campground, the road crosses into North Carolina (Mile 473).

U.S. Route 21 in North Carolina

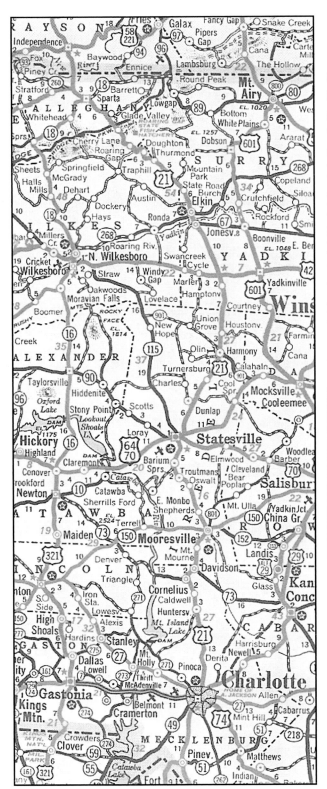

When formed in 1926, Route 21 shared the path of North Carolina state Route 26, which was originally a three-state road, also existing as state Route 26 in Virginia and South Carolina. This extra numerical designation had been eliminated by 1933. Once in North Carolina, the fourth of five states through which Route 21 originally traveled, the road enters Alleghany County, named for the Allegheny Mountain range that actually lies considerably north of this region. The name is derived from a Delaware Indian word for "fine river"; interestingly, "Allegheny" is the French spelling and "Allegany" is the English spelling, and there are numerous variations on both as the name shows up in various places throughout Appalachia.

Upon crossing the state line, Route 21 continues past the New River Campground; three

(left) Gulf gasoline roadmap from 1936, showing U.S. 21 through North Carolina; (above) State line as seen in 1994 [photo by Tim Murphy]; (below) Kelly's Motel operated in Sparta, as seen here in the 1950s.

87

Charles' Motel, Sparta, N. C.

(left) Charles' Motel operated at the northwest corner of North Main and Charles Streets in Sparta; although closed, the building remains standing today; (below right) Alleghany County courthouse at the corner of Routes 21 and 18 in the center of Sparta.

miles south of this, it reaches the unincorporated community of Twin Oaks, where Route 221 heads west and 21 turns east (left). Although there is just one store and gas station today at the junction, it was once the site of a three-story hotel, built in the late 1920s and operated by Carl Irwin, who also had rental cabins across the road. The hotel and cab-ins had closed by the 1970s and had been razed by the mid-1990s. There was also a drive-in movie theater where two large oak trees had stood that gave the village its name. Another three miles brings the road to the town of Sparta, the county seat, with its population of just over 1,800; here the road becomes North Main Street for a brief stretch before reaching the center of town at the intersection with Whitehead Street (Mile 479). At the northeast corner of this intersection is the Alleghany County courthouse, built in 1910 and then rebuilt after being gutted by a fire in 1933. It is listed on the National

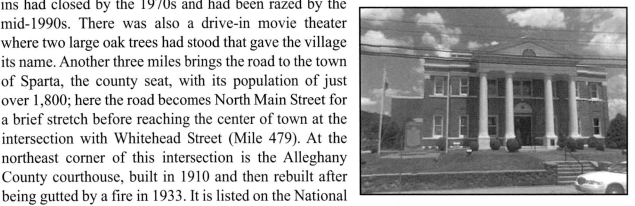

Register of Historic Places. Whitehead Street carries state Route 18, which travels more than 100 miles through the mountains of western North Carolina from Lowgap to Earl. South of the inter-

section, Route 21 becomes South Main Street until leaving the town limits upon crossing the Little River, a tributary of the New River.

Continuing south, the next stretch of the road had several reroutings over the years, mostly in the 1930s, with most of the original alignments still visible. The first is two miles out of Sparta, where State Road 1119, also known as "Old 21," travels south of the current road, reconnecting to it a mile later. Shortly thereafter, the road goes through the unincorporated locality of Glade Valley, named for the Glade Creek nearby. Most of the community lies a half-mile to the east of Route 21, and although very small, it does have its own post office and zip code. The road then continues south through another rural stretch before reaching the entrance to the Blue Ridge Parkway. The parkway is a National Scenic Byway, established in the 1930s, which stretches 469 miles from the Great Smoky Mountains National Park in North Carolina to Waynesboro, Virginia, where it connects to the

(above left) Marions Roaring Gap Motel and Restaurant, seen in the 1950s, stood two miles south of the Blue Ridge Parkway; (right) Gas station in Roaring Gap, circa 1930s.

(left) The High Meadows Inn in Roaring Gap, as seen in the 1970s; it remains in business today, located near the entrance to the High Meadows Golf and Country Club; (below) View of the distant Piedmont Region from the Olde Beau golf club.

Skyline Drive, another National Scenic Byway. Shortly after passing under the large stone bridge that carries the parkway, Route 21 travels through the unincorporated village of Cherry Lane (Mile 488). In this area, another brief section of the route's original alignment can be seen on the west side of the road as State Road 1107, or Foxfire Road.

Two more miles brings the road into Roaring Gap, another unincorporated village, albeit one with its own post office and zip code, and a population of 142. Originally known as Laurel Branch, it was supposedly renamed for the sound of wind blowing through the mountains, and was established in the 1890s as a summer resort by Alexander Chatham, who owned a textile mill in nearby Elkin. The area has been home to several youth camps over the years, including the YMCA's Camp Cheerio, a popular site which remains in operation today. Three exclusive golf communities are in Roaring Gap (all located along Route 21), the oldest of which is the Roaring Gap Club, a descendent of the original resort. It is centered around Greystone Inn, a large struc-

ture that opened in 1926. Also part of the grounds of the club is Lake Louise, the site of a former girl scout camp, which lies directly along Route 21 just north of the club's entrance. Also on the east side of the road is the newer Olde Beau Golf Club, opened in 1991 on the site of the former mountain retreat of Winston Salem industrialist R. J. Reynolds. On the west side of the road is the High Meadows Golf and Country Club, which opened in 1964.

Immediately south of the entrance to the Roaring Gap Club is the Eastern Continental Divide, which is listed as being at an elevation of 2,972 feet. This is a line running generally north and south, east of which all bodies of water drain into the Atlantic Ocean, and west of which all bodies of water drain into the Mississippi River watershed and the Gulf of Mexico. Also in this area, there are two additional sites where the road has been rerouted; the first is across from the entrance to Olde Beau Golf Club, where Green House Road veers off to the west of the main road, curving back to meet it less than a mile later. The next site is immediately past Lake Louise, where a narrow driveway curves to the east of the road, rejoining it shortly thereafter and crossing back across the road. Over the next mile, there are six sepa-

rate intersections with the original alignment, which was very curvy throughout this section around the site of the Continental Divide, and it eventually traveled west of the main route onto State Road 1100, known variously as Stone Mountain Road, Old Gap Road, and Oklahoma Road. After a mile or so of sharp

Greystone Inn, opened in 1926 and located on the grounds of the Roaring Gap Club.

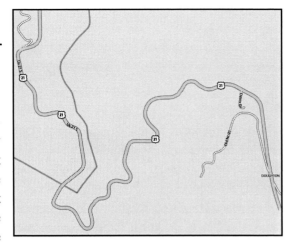

curves on this road, Route 21 rejoined the current alignment before descending the upcoming hill. Exactly when the route was straightened to its current alignment is unclear; county maps from the 1930s do not show the road clearly enough to tell, although it appears that much of the realignment was done between the late 1920s and late 1930s. The previously mentioned Stone Mountain Road travels approximately five miles to Stone Mountain State Park, which covers more than 13,000 acres centered around a 600-foot high dome of exposed granite. This is one of the most popular sites in the region for rock climbing.

Back on Route 21, south of Stone Mountain Road, the route begins a long descent from the high ground on the ridge, dropping from nearly 3,000 feet to around 1,200 feet over the next seven miles. The numerous sharp curves along the way are reminiscent of the route's trek over East River and Big Walker Mountains in Virginia, and its original alignment down the hill was reminiscent of the Raleigh-Grayson Turnpike through that same area, with many sharp curves. The original road up the hill was more winding, and portions of it were rebuilt in the 1940s and again in the 1950s to straighten it to some extent. Sections of the original alignment can still be

seen via satellite views, while others have disappeared over the years. Approximately two miles down the hill, the road crosses into Wilkes County, and just past this, there is a scenic overlook on the south side of the road, from which a dramatic view of the state's Piedmont Region can be seen.

At the bottom of the hill, the road goes through the unincorporated locality of Doughton. At this point, the original alignment joins the main highway from the west as State Road 1733, or "N Old Highway 21." The modern alignment travels south from here, curving east and just south of Thurmond and continuing on a fairly straight course over the next ten miles on its way to Elkin, crossing into Surry County and then traveling through the unincorporated village of State Road along the way. This entire section replaced the original alignment in the mid-1950s. The original routing also went south out of Doughton, then curved north on State Road 1901 (Thurmond Post Office Road) and into the unincorporated village of Thurmond (Mile 498), at an elevation of 1,400 feet. The old road then travels east from Thurmond on State Road 1902, or Thurmond Road, somewhat north of modern Route 21. It crosses the modern route about two miles further along, traveling then on the south side as State Road 2070, or "Old Highway 21". This reconnects to the current road at State Road, but shortly thereafter, State Road 1161, or Klondike Road, is another portion of the original alignment that travels south of the modern road for another two miles before reconnecting just west of the junction with the Route 21 bypass around Elkin.

At this point, the road splits into modern Route 21 and Business Route 21. The former is

(right) The Hugh G. Chatham Bridge over the Yadkin River, named after the owner of the Chatham Manufacturing Company, a local textile mill that has been one of the area's largest employers for a century; built in 1931, the bridge is on Gwyn Street and is currently condemned.

a four-lane bypass of the original road around the towns of Elkin and Jonesville; Business 21 is the old road. Opened in 1965, the modern road travels for two miles before connecting with Interstate 77, with which it shares the highway over the next four miles before 21 reconnects to the old road and continues south. Meanwhile, Business 21 curves to the south at this point, into the locality of Elkin Valley, where it is known as North Bridge Street. This stretch of 21 through the northern part of Elkin is a very commercial district, with many new stores appearing in recent years. Just past a Wal Mart plaza, the original alignment of the road curves to the east as State Road 1146, or North Elkin Drive. This runs parallel to the modern road and reconnects to it one mile south. Three miles along Business 21, the road reaches downtown Elkin (Mile 510) at the intersection with state Route 268, which travels more than eighty miles from Lenoir to Moores Springs in the state's Piedmont region. At the southeast corner of Bridge and Main Streets is the Twenty-One & Main restaurant, an upscale establishment with its own wine bar for sampling the products from local wineries, of which there are at least a dozen. Continuing south, the road crosses the Yadkin River, at which point the road enters Yadkin County and the town of Jonesville, with its population of nearly 1,500 (although in 2001 it merged with the neighboring town of Arlington, increasing the town's official population to more than 2,200).

The Yadkin River is a tributary of the Pee Dee River, which travels southeast to enter the Atlantic Ocean at Georgetown, South Carolina; it is the first body of water traveling south along Route 21 to drain into the ocean. Two bridges cross the river to connect Elkin and Jonesville; an original narrow bridge along Bridge Street in Elkin carried the route until the early 1940s, when the routing was moved to the Hugh G. Chatham Bridge (built in 1931) along Gwyn Avenue, one block to the east. At that time, the route turned east from Bridge Street onto Market Street for one block before turning south on Gwyn and then continuing south on Bridge Street in Jonesville. After the original bridge was replaced in 1970, the route returned to Bridge Street, where it currently remains (the Chatham Bridge is now condemned). After crossing the river today, Route 21 turns east on Elm Street, then south one block later on Bridge Street in Jonesville to continue south.

One block further south, the road intersects state Route 67, which begins at this point and travels nearly sixty miles east to Winston-Salem. The road then continues south through Jonesville, and after passing Valley Drive, it enters the town of Arlington (Mile

Two older views of the Rose Village Motel in Jonesville, which remains in business today at the southwest corner of Routes 21 and 67, two blocks south of the Chatham Bridge. In the bottom photo, a sign for Route 21 can be seen at lower left.

**COUNTRY INN — JONESVILLE
NORTH CAROLINA**

(left) The Country Inn, northwest of the junction of Routes 21 and 77 south of Arlington, as seen in 1988; it remains in operation today as an America's Best Value Inn; (below right) Modern map of Routes 21 and 77 from Elkin south, showing several reroutings of 21: around Elkin, away from Mooresville and Davidson near Lake Norman, and onto the interstate while passing through Charlotte to the state line; (bottom left) The Bell Motor Court just north of the intersection of Route 21 and Old 421; it remains in business today as apartments.

512), where it is renamed as North Main Street. Arlington had a population around 800 until 2001 when, as previous noted, it merged with Jonesville. Upon passing Center Street, the road becomes South Main Street and soon passes out of town and back into a fairly rural setting. Just over a mile further south, the road crosses I-77 at Exit 79, at which point modern Route 21 exits the interstate to continue south on its original course, while Business Route 21 comes to an end.

Now running east of the interstate, the road continues south for another six miles through mostly rural countryside, passing through the localities of Rena, Wagoner, and Longtown before coming to the unincorporated community of Brooks Cross Roads. This is at the intersection with Old U.S. Route 421, another spur of Route 21 which travels nearly 1,000 miles from Michigan City, Indiana, along Lake Michigan, to Fort Fisher, near Wilmington, N.C. Just south of this intersection, 21 crosses modern Route 421, which is a standard four-lane divided highway. Next, the road travels through the unincorporated area of Hamptonville (Mile 521), which is classified as a census-designated place, with a population of 5,901. This includes the entire area within its zip code, not just the small area along Route 21. Two more miles brings the road through the locality of Lone Hickory before the road enters into Iredell County. At this point, the road officially leaves the Appalachian region (see the Ohio chapter), which stretches as far south as Yadkin County.

Upon entering Iredell County, the road is known as Harmony Highway, and three miles later it passes through the locality of Houstonville. Another four miles brings the road into the town of Harmony (Mile 531), with its population of just over 500. On the south side of Harmony, the road crosses state Route 901, which travels from Union Grove in western Iredell County to a junction with U.S. Route 64 in Davie County. Just south of this, 21 is renamed as Turnersburg Highway, and four miles further along, it enters the unin-

Bell Motor Court

BROOKS CROSS ROADS, N.C.

corporated community of Turnersburg, just as the road crosses Rocky Creek, a tributary of the Yadkin River. At this point, a brief, half-mile segment of the original alignment can be seen to the east of the highway, where an older bridge across the creek once stood. When the current bridge was built in the early 1980s, the road was rerouted slightly west, the old bridge was razed, and the original segment of the road was abandoned. Continuing south from here, the road soon crosses the South Fork of the Yadkin River. It then continues south through a sparsely populated rural area before intersecting I-77

again, at Exit 54. Just before the exit is the Statesville Auto Auction, a huge site for resale of used cars and one of the county's largest employers. Continuing past the interstate, the area gradually becomes more populated and commercial as it enters the

outskirts of the city of Statesville. This trend continues until the road reaches a fairly congested area of restaurants and motels at Exit 151 of Interstate 40, a major east-west highway which travels more than 2,500 miles from Wilmington, N.C. to Barstow, California. South of this, the road enters the city of Statesville, where it is named as Sullivan Road.

Statesville is the Iredell County seat, with a population of more than 23,300, and with its origin in the 1750s, it is one of the oldest towns in the region. Sullivan Road continues south for a mile beyond the interstate before ending at Davie Avenue where it bears to the right (southwest) and heads into the downtown area. Davie Avenue also carries U.S. Route 64, which travels more than 2,300 miles from Nags Head, N.C. to

Arizona near Four Corners. After another mile, Davie Avenue ends on North Tradd Street, with Routes 21 and 64 turning left onto that and continuing another two blocks before turning right onto East Front Street. Two blocks later, the route reaches the center of town (Mile 547) at South Center Street, where 21 turns left to continue south, while Route 64 continues west out

(above right) Aerial view of the city of Statesville; (above) Old City Hall building at the northeast corner of Center and Front Streets; (right) The Vance Hotel, built in 1922, stands across the street from the Old City Hall.

93

(left) Two of the city's many motels, as seen in the early 1960s; the top one is the Statesville Motor Lodge, on the north side of the junction of Route 21 and I-40; (below) The Presbyterian Orphans' Home as seen in the 1940s; the complex straddles Route 21 and operates today as the Barium Springs Home For Children; the Woman's Building still stands today along with mostly newer buildings.

of the city. Center also carries state Route 115, which travels from North Wilkesboro to Charlotte and also carries much of the original alignment of 21 closer to Charlotte. After traveling three blocks on South Center, 21 and 115 bear to the right onto Shelton Avenue, which then carries both out of the city. Several blocks south of this, the road crosses Industrial Boulevard, which also carries the modern routing of U.S. Route 70. This is another major east-west highway that travels more than 2,300 miles from the ocean in Atlantic, N.C. west to Arizona, although until 1964 it continued west into Los Angeles. Until the construction of Industrial Boulevard, the route crossed 21 at Broad Street in the downtown district. 21 continues south from this point and soon leaves the city, passing back into a semi-rural area. A very early alignment of the road curved three blocks to the west in the area of Industrial Boulevard, using Old Charlotte Road and 4th Street, and eventually reconnecting to the modern routing. When the original lay-out of the U.S. Route System was being established in 1926, one proposed routing of 21 from Statesville took it east to Salisbury along modern U.S. 70, then south on U.S. 29 through Concord and into Charlotte on North Tryon Street. While this alignment appears on at least one map from the era, it does not appear that the route ever actually followed this path.

Once passing out of the city, another segment of the road's original alignment can be seen, curving to the east as Cumberland Road, and reconnecting to the modern road after a mile. The modern road then passes through the unincorporated locality of Barium Springs, named for nine springs in the area that were discovered by early settlers in the 1700s. The spring water had a large mineral content, with one particular spring containing barium; the water was bottled and sold throughout the country in the 1800s for its supposed healthful effects, and a thirty-room hotel was established at the site. This continued to operate into the early 1900s, after which the land was sold to the Presbyterian church, which moved its orphanage to the site. The orphanage, founded in Charlotte in 1883, occupies several buildings on both sides of Route 21 and at one time operated its own farm, dairy, orchard, laundry, print shop and other functions at the site. It continues to operate today as the Barium Springs Home For Children, and offers services to more than 2,000 young people annually.

As the road continues south, it soon reaches the town of Troutman (Mile 552), with its population of nearly 1,600. Like Statesville, Troutman was founded in the 1750s, and took

(right) Postcard from Davidson, showing an overview of Lake Norman with local scenes and roads; (below) View of the lake from Cowans Ford Dam.

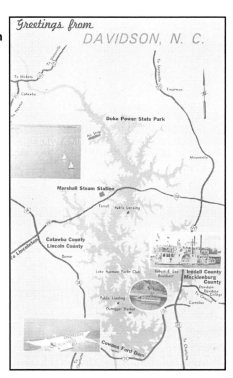

its name from an early settler whose name was actually Trautman. Route 21 is named as North and then South Main Street through the town. Traveling parallel to the road on its east side through much of the town are North and South Eastway Drive, which appear to have been an early alignment of state Route 26, the road's pre-1926 title; it appears that this alignment had been abandoned, however, by the time that U.S. 21 was established. Upon leaving Troutman, the road passes through the locality of Oswalt before crossing I-77 again at Exit 42. At one time, the entire twelve-mile section of modern I-77 from Exits 42 to 54 was proposed to be used as a Route 21 bypass of Statesville, similar to the bypass around Elkin, but in the end the old routing through the city was maintained.

Passing south of the interstate, the road is known as Charlotte Highway, and travels through an area that until recently was mostly rural, but in recent years has seen the construction of numerous housing developments along Route 21 as the area around Mooresville and the entire greater Charlotte region have seen continued population growth. After passing through the unincorporated locality of Shepherds, the road splits into its modern and original (now numbered as state Route 115) alignments, which do not overlap again until reaching South Carolina. Following the modern alignment first, it bears to the right at the split and continues south and to the west of the original route, bypassing the towns of Mooresville, Davidson, Cornelius, and Huntersville. Opened in the mid-1950s, the new road was built for more efficient travel and is somewhat less scenic than the original road. The new routing of 21 was later incorporated into the construction of I-77 when that road was completed through the region in 1975, in order to utilize two long bridges over Lake Norman for both routes. Three miles south of the split with Route 115, the modern road crosses state Route 150, which travels from Yanceyville near the Virginia line to the South Carolina line west of Charlotte. Three miles further south, the road comes to a junction with I-77, at Exit 33. Here, 21 crosses the interstate and turns left onto its entrance ramp, sharing the road for the next five miles. This section of the interstate was originally part of the new routing of 21, although a very brief section of the pre-interstate routing runs south of the exit as Fairview Road (which leads to the modern Lake Norman Regional Medical Center, around the corner).

Once on the interstate, the road crosses two separate sections of Lake Norman as it travels through the western edges of the towns of Davidson and Cornelius. Lake Norman was estab-

lished between 1959 and 1964 after the construction of the Cowans Ford Dam along the Catawba River. The dam was built by Duke Power (the region's largest electricity producer, now known as Duke Energy) in conjunction with the construction of the McGuire nuclear power plant, which opened in the early 1980s, adjacent to the dam. Both are located approximately ten miles west of downtown Huntersville, and currently provide power to much of western North Carolina. With over 500 miles of

(left) Aerial view of downtown Charlotte in the 1960s; (below left) Charlotte skyline as of 2008; with the recent appearance of multiple skyscrapers and other large complexes, the city continues to emerge as one of the fastest growing areas in the country, both physically and economically; (below right) Bank of America Stadium [photo taken by by Captain Wayne Capps, USAF].

shoreline, the lake has led to a dramatic change in the landscape of the region in recent years–many formerly rural areas have become expensive residential neighborhoods, both for vacation and primary homes, and this has helped to greatly enlarge the greater Charlotte region, both in size and population. As an example, looking at the populations of three towns adjacent to Lake Norman before and after its formation, Mooresville had population of 5,600 in 1934, compared to 18,800 today. Davidson has gone from 1,445 to 7,100 in the same period, and Cornelius has gone from 1,230 to nearly 12,000. Fishing and boating are plentiful on the lake, and marinas and many private docks are visible when crossing it on Route 21.

South of the lake, the area is highly commercialized with motels, strip malls, and various businesses all along the road. Route 21 leaves the interstate at Exit 28 in the locality of Smithville, traveling just to the east on Catawba Avenue and then south on Statesville Road, parallel to and within site of the interstate. Three miles further south, the road crosses state Route 73, which travels more than 100 miles from Lincolnton to Pinehurst. At the northeast corner of this intersection (on the western edge of the town of Huntersville) is the Northcross Shopping Center, one of the largest retail complexes in the area. Continuing another six miles south through this mostly commercial district, the road crosses Interstate 485, an outerbelt that encircles the city of Charlotte (although it is currently unfinished, with one six-mile stretch east of this still unbuilt). One more mile south, the road crosses state Route 24, which travels nearly 300 miles from this point east to Morehead City. Statesville Road then continues another two miles south before again intersecting state Route 115 (Old 21), which ends at this point. Although Statesville Road continues south from this point, the modern routing of 21 takes it a half-mile west on Sunset Road to rejoin I-77 at Exit 16, in the locality of Trinity. From this point south to just beyond the South Carolina state line, Routes 21 and 77 share the road, bypassing downtown Charlotte. This rerouting process took place between 1969 and 1987, as more sections of 21 were gradually routed onto the interstate, until the current alignment was achieved.

Three miles further south, 21/77 crosses Interstate 85, a major route that travels more than 600 miles from Montgomery, AL. to Petersburg, VA. Two miles later at Exit 11, it crosses Interstate 277, a four-mile loop around downtown that reconnects to 21/77 two miles south. This is

96

known as the Brookshire Freeway and also carries state Route 16, which travels from the Virginia state line in the western part of the state to Waxhaw, near the South Carolina border. South of this, the road passes the city's main downtown district, and two miles later, the road crosses West Morehead Street, which carries state Route 27, traveling 200 miles from Toluca in the western part of the state to Benson in the eastern part of the state. Morehead also carries U.S. Route 29, which travels more than 1,000 miles from Baltimore, MD. to Pensacola, FL. From this exit, one can see the Bank of America Stadium several blocks to the east. Opened in 1996, it seats more than 73,000 fans and is home to the NFL Carolina Panthers football team. Just south of this is a large intersection with the southern part of I-277 and U.S. 74, which travels more than 500 miles from the Atlantic Ocean at Wrightsville Beach, N.C. to Chattanooga, TN. This is also known as the Belk Freeway and the Andrew Jackson Highway. Another mile south, the road crosses state Route 160, which has a relatively brief course through greater Charlotte. Routes 21/77 then continue through suburban Charlotte, crossing South Tryon Street at Exit 6; this carries state Route 49, which travels from the South Carolina state line near here to the Virginia state line north of Roxboro. At the same exit, the road crosses the Billy Graham Parkway and East Woodlawn Road, both of which carry U.S. Route 521, another spur of 21 which travels from Charlotte east to Georgetown, S.C. Four miles south of that, the road crosses I-485 again as it is passing south of the city. Routes 21/77 then leave the city limits, and two more miles brings the road to the South Carolina state line, where it continues south in the next chapter.

Returning to the split north of Mooresville, we now follow the original alignment of Route 21 through the area. Bearing to the left at the split, it continues south as Statesville Highway, or state Route 115. After two miles it crosses state Route 150 and and becomes North Broad Street as it enters the town of Mooresville. Mooresville is known as Race City, U.S.A. due to it being home to numerous NASCAR teams as well as the NASCAR Technical Institute, the North Carolina Auto Racing Hall of Fame, and drivers Dale Earnhardt, Jr. and Kasey Kahne. As the area becomes more commercial, the road bears right at West Statesville Avenue (which despite the name is not an older alignment of the route) and continues south on North Broad into the downtown district (Mile 562). At Iredell Avenue, the road crosses state Routes 152 (traveling from here east to Rockwell) and 3 (traveling from here south to Concord) before continuing south,

paralleling the main line of railroad tracks that splits the town from north to south. The downtown retains many of its older buildings that give it a traditional small-town atmosphere. At McLelland Avenue, the route turns left (east) to cross the tracks before turning immediately to the right (south) on South Main Street, directly across the tracks from Broad Street. It then continues south out of town and back into a somewhat rural setting, becoming the Mecklenburg Highway after leaving the town limits.

Two miles beyond the town limits, the road

(above left) The Carolina Inn, built around 1848, was a store and hotel along Old 21, across from the Davidson College campus; today it is owned by the college and is part of the campus; (left) Chambers Building, the central point on campus, was built in 1929 and houses the majority of classrooms and faculty offices.

(right) Eumenean Hall, built in 1849, housed the Eumenean Debating Society, and stands facing a similar building, Philanthropic Hall; both buildings are listed on the National Register of Historic Places; (below right) Davidson College Presbyterian Church stands near the center of campus; built in 1952 to replace an older structure, the church seats 1,200.

reaches the unincorporated community of Mount Mourne, at which point it is only a half-mile east of the modern routing of 21 and 77. This area is also home to the headquarters of the Lowe's Home Improvement Warehouse chain, which is just east of the road at this point, off of East Campus Lane. Two miles beyond this, the road enters Mecklenburg County, the last and largest (with a population of more than 900,000) of the six counties through which Route 21 travels in the state. Here, it also enters the town of Davidson (Mile 569), at which point the road becomes known as North Main Street. Founded in the 1830s and named after a local Revolutionary War hero, the town is best known as the home of Davidson College, through which the road passes on the town's north side. Established in 1837 by a Presbyterian group, Davidson has approximately 1,700 undergraduate students, and is consistently one of the nation's highest rated liberal arts colleges. The central part of its campus lies on the east side of Route 115/Old 21 in this area; in the old days, students supposedly referred to the road as the "Red Sea," as they had to cross a sea of the local reddish-brown muddy clay to get to a store on the other side.

Back on the road, Route 115/Old 21 bears to the right in the center of picturesque Davidson, continuing as South Main Street before leaving the town and entering the adjacent town of Cornelius. Being renamed as North Main Street again upon reaching Cornelius, the road quickly goes through the small, commercial downtown area; most of the recent growth in the town has been west of here along I-77, where many motels and restaurants have appeared, and further west along the shoreline of Lake Norman, where numerous upscale residential areas have developed. Upon heading south out of the town, Route 115 goes from the name of South Main Street to Old Statesville Road. Continuing south through the unincorporated locality of Caldwell, the road then enters the town of Huntersville (Mile 576), with its population of nearly 25,000, where it soon crosses state Route 73. Another suburb of Charlotte that has seen tremendous growth in recent years, Huntersville has a miminal downtown area, with most of its growth being to the west along the interstate and closer to Lake Norman. On the south side of town, the road passes

(left) Map of Route 21 through Charlotte in 1958 (when its population was 165,000); the road has since been routed entirely onto I-77 through this area, bypassing the downtown district altogether.

98

the north campus of Central Piedmont Community College, one of the college's eight campuses in the greater Charlotte area. Founded in1963, the college has over 1,600 students. Further south, the road crosses the entrance to I-485, the outer belt around Charlotte. As previously mentioned, the road is currently unfinished and starts at this point going west and then south, with its end point six miles east of here. The road then continues through an increasingly commercial stretch near the locality of Croft before crossing state Route 24, and two miles south of this point, it reaches the intersection with the modern alignment of Route 21. Old Statesville Road and Route 115 both end at this point, as the modern alignment turns west on Sunset Road to join I-77. From here south, the original alignment continues south on Statesville Road, with no numbered route designation from here into Charlotte.

The road continues through a typical suburban setting, and three miles further south it crosses I-85 at Exit 39. By this time, the road has entered into the city of Charlotte, the state's largest city, with a recent population estimate of over 687,000; its metropolitan area has a population of more than 1.7 million. Charlotte was the nation's eighteenth-largest city as of 2008. First settled in 1755, the city later took its name from Princess Charlotte of Mecklenburg, who married King George III in 1761 to become the Queen Consort of England. The city (and surrounding area) has seen significant growth in the past twenty years, with no slowdown in sight. Back on Old 21, the road passes through several neighborhoods on the city's north side, such as Wilson Heights, Double Oaks, and Lockwood, as it draws closer to the downtown area. South of the intersection with Lasalle Street (roughly two miles north of downtown), the city's skyline becomes readily visible in the distance. Standing out in particular is the city's tallest building, the Bank of America Corporate Center, completed in 1992. Standing 871 feet tall, it has sixty floors and is the state's tallest building as well as being the tallest between Philadelphia and Atlanta. Statesville Avenue soon ends at North Graham Street, where Old 21 turns right to join with U.S. Route 29 and state Route 49. Shortly after this, the road passes under the Brookshire Freeway, carrying I-277 and state Route 16 before continuing into the downtown area (Mile 590). Several blocks beyond this, just south of West Sixth Street, the road passes the large, modern Charlotte Cotton Mill apartment complex, built adjacent to the former Camden Cotton Mill, built in 1881 and facing Graham Street.

Route 21 followed three separate alignments through Charlotte at different times: the original one in the 1920s was a complicated, zigzag arrangement that began on North Graham, turning left onto West Trade Street, then right on South Mint Street, left on West 1st Street, right on South Tryon Street, left on East Morehead Street, and finally right on South Boulevard to head south out of the city. By 1930, the alignment had been simplified slightly, with the

(top left) Charlotte skyline at night, with the Bank of America building standing out; (above left) View of the Bank of America Stadium from South Graham Street.

route turning left from North Graham onto West 11th Street (at the modern site of the Brookshire Freeway), then right on North Tryon Street, left on East Morehead, and right on South Boulevard. In the late 1930s, the route was further simplified, with Route 21 continuing on South Graham until turning left onto West Morehead (at the modern site of the Bank of America Stadium), then right on South Boulevard. This latter alignment, which bypasses the more congested central business district, remained in place until the route was moved onto the interstate more than thirty years later [thanks again to Michael Roberson of NCRoads.com for his extensive research on this subject]. In the 1990s, South Graham was routed one block east onto South Mint Street at the site of the new football stadium, so that following Old 21 requires using Mint Street for one block to reach Morehead. The route reaches this intersection almost

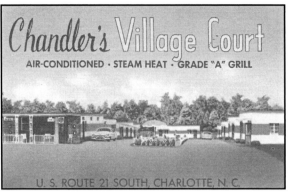

immediately after passing under the Belk Freeway, carrying I-277 and U.S. Route 74. Upon reaching Morehead, Route 29 turns right to travel west, while Old 21 and Route 49 turn left onto Morehead, which also carries state Route 27.

Roughly a half-mile southeast on Morehead Street, the road intersects South Boulevard, which carries Old 21 out of the city. However, in recent years, Morehead has been routed over South Blvd. in order to allow the latter to have access to I-277, with no direct access between the two. Therefore, the easiest way to trace Old 21 is to turn right (south) onto South Tryon Street prior to reaching South Blvd. After one block on Tryon, a left turn onto Carson Boulevard then leads to South Blvd., where a right turn continues to follow Old 21. Over the next eight miles, the road continues through an increasingly suburban area as it leaves the city, roughly at the southern crossing of the I-485 outerbelt. In doing so, Old 21 passes through several more neighborhoods such as South End, Sedgefield, Collingwood, Madison Park, Starmount, and Sterling. It also travels parallel to a former line of the Norfolk Southern Railway, which in recent years has been converted into a light rail system that travels

from downtown south to the city limits. The rail line runs west of Old 21, in some places directly adjacent to the road. Just north of Clanton Road, Old 21 splits into two one-way sections, with the southbound lanes

(above) View of the 21 South drive-in #2 on Independence Blvd., which is virtually identical to the original location and remains in business today, with its original neon sign [photo courtesy of Michael Hale]; (left) New sign at the original location on South Blvd. (now closed) after the first one was destroyed by Hurricane Hugo in 1989.

crossing the railroad tracks and continuing on their west side, with the northbound lanes remaining on the east side of the tracks. This arrangement continues for a half-mile before the southbound lanes cross the tracks again to rejoin the northbound lanes. The next intersection after this is for State Road 1308, or Old Pineville Road, which was the original alignment of 21 from this point to Pineville. It was rerouted onto modern South Blvd. in the mid-1930s.

On the east side of the road in this same area, at 3627 South Blvd., is one prominent local vestige of the past: the 21 South drive-in restaurant. Opened in December 1954 by Sam, George, and Nick Copsis, three Greek immigrant brothers, the restaurant was one of several such drive-ins along the course of Route 21, although it was the only one known to incorporate the road's name into its own. At the time of its opening, it was located at the southern limits of suburban Charlotte's development, and because more space was available in this area, a parking lot was built that could accomodate up to fifty-four cars. The rapid success of the restaurant led to the opening of a second location on Independence Blvd. in 1959, and a third one on North Tryon Street shortly thereafter. After more than fifty years of business at the site (owned and operated by the Copsis family throughout that time), the original location (and the company's namesake) closed in 2007, a victim of slowing business due to competition from other nearby restaurants. Business also suffered when South Blvd. was divided as previously described, as part of the conversion of the railroad tracks to the light rail line; this greatly limited drivers' access to the restaurant. Although empty, the building remains standing as of 2010, and four other 21 South restaurants remain open in the area.

Continuing south, the road soon crosses Woodlawn Road, where U.S. 521 joins the road going south for the next five miles, before it joins in with I-485 to continue southeast toward Georgetown, S.C. At the point of this intersection, South Blvd. has left the city limits and is briefly renamed as Pineville Road, just prior to entering the town of Pineville, with its population of more than 4,200. This area has seen tremendous commercial growth in recent years, due largely to the construction of the interstate through the area. Upon entering the town, Old 21 becomes known as North Polk Street, which continues into the small, original downtown district (Mile 601). Here, Old 21 turns right onto Main Street, which today is numbered as state Route 51, traveling from Mint Hill to the South Carolina state line. Just a half-mile south of here on South Polk Street is the site of the birthplace of the town's most famous resident, James K. Polk, the eleventh President of the United States. His father Samuel Polk was a farmer and slaveholder and one of the earliest settlers in the area. The log farmhouse where Polk was born in 1795 is no longer standing, but a similar building from that time period was moved to the historical site as a representation of the original home. A visitor center and small museum also stand at the site.

Continuing west on Main Street, Old 21 quickly leaves the downtown area and becomes known as Rock Hill-Pineville Road. The road rapidly returns to a very rural setting for the first time in many miles, and less than two miles later it reaches the South Carolina state line, where it continues south in the following chapter.

James K. Polk and the log structure representing his birthplace in Pineville

101

U.S. Route 21 in South Carolina

Prior to 1926, most of the series of roads that make up Route 21 in South Carolina were originally numbered as state Route 26, as in Virginia and North Carolina. Of the five states through which 21 passes, it spends the most time in South Carolina, with 224 miles of road, although it has been lengthened from its original 1926 layout. Initially ending at U.S. Route 17 near Yemassee, it was extended to Beaufort in 1935, and then extended to Hunting Island at the Atlantic Ocean in 1954. As mentioned in the introduction, the original proposed routing of 21 took it south along U.S. 17 from Yemassee through Georgia and eventually to Jacksonville, Florida, although that southernmost segment of the route was never implemented.

Upon crossing into South Carolina and York County, there is still a division between modern 21, which continues to follow Interstate 77 at the state line, and "Old 21," which follows modern state Route 51 just west of Pineville, North Carolina. 21 was routed off of this road and onto what is now the interstate in 1968. Modern 21 leaves the interstate at Exit 90, the first exit in the state, just one mile across the state line. Going south from here, it almost immediately meets up with Old 21/Route 51 coming from Pineville, and the modern road then continues south on its original alignment. At this same exit from the interstate, the road going north is named as Carowinds Blvd., leading to the entrance of Carowinds amusement park. Carowinds opened in 1973 and is unique in the fact that the park straddles the state line, with half in one state and half in the other (similar to the former Ridge Runner railroad ride on the

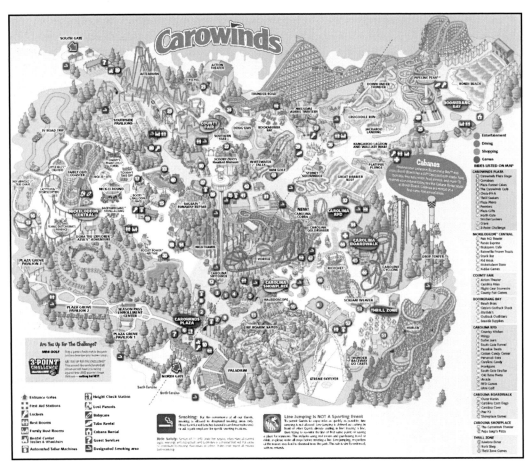

Carowinds park map; note the state line dividing the entrance in half.

Heritage, U.S.A.

One of the more notorious sites along Route 21 was the Heritage U.S.A. theme park, a branch of the PTL ("Praise The Lord"or "People That Love") Club, a popular television ministry in the 1980s. Founded by Jim and Tammy Bakker, the ministry had a multitude of followers around the world, and in 1978, it opened a Christianity-based theme park, water park, and resort near Fort Mill. In addition to having the PTL headquarters and television studios at the site, there was also a 500-room hotel, campground, indoor shopping complex, and other amenities. By the mid-1980s, it employed 2,500 people and had nearly six million visitors annually, making it the country's third-most popular vacation destination (behind Disneyland and Disney World).

The complex continued to grow with the construction of the Heritage Towers, a 21-story addition to the hotel. This huge project was never finished, however, as the PTL began to have financial problems in the late 1980s, coupled with news of Bakker's involvement with church employee Jessica Hahn that led to a rapid drop in park attendance along with its sale to Jerry Falwell in 1987. With the PTL heavily in debt, the theme park was then damaged by Hurricane Hugo in 1989, and it closed soon thereafter. Parts of the huge site remain functional today, such as the main hotel and the broadcast facility, while others remain standing and unused, like the Heritage Towers, which remains empty with its windows all broken, a testament to the rapid rise and fall of a televangelism empire.

(top left) Sign at the entrance to the park; (top right) Jim and Tammy Faye in better times; (above left) Entrance to the Heritage Grand Hotel, which remains standing today and is used by the MorningStar Ministries; (above right) Artist's rendition of the 21-story Heritage Towers building, which was never finished and remains standing today in various stages of decay.

WV/VA border). With fifty rides throughout the park, it is owned by the Cedar Fair Company, owner of Ohio's Cedar Point amusement park, and it remains a popular entertainment spot in the greater Charlotte area.

Back on 21, less than a mile past the point where Old and Modern 21 rejoin, the road splits again at the locality of Forest Lake, with Business Route 21 (known variously as Charlotte Highway or Old Nation Road) following the original course through the town of Fort Mill, while

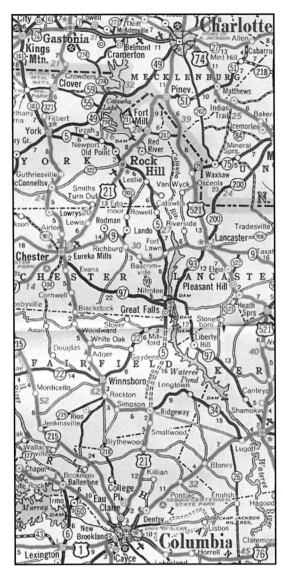

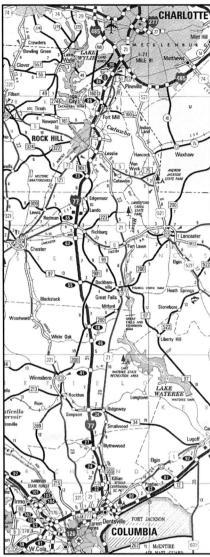

Bypass 21 (which opened in 1948) travels west of the town over seven miles of unremarkable rural territory before rejoining the original road. Meanwhile, after the split, Business 21 soon encounters Heritage Blvd., which travels to the east and into the former site of the Heritage U.S.A. theme park (see box), which stood less than a mile east of 21. Old Nation Road then continues south through a mix of rural and residential territory before entering the town of Fort Mill, with its population of nearly 7,600 (although the surrounding township has a population of around 35,000). Old Nation Road ends at North White Street, which also carries state Route 160, a short route running from just east of here north to the state line. 21 turns left (south) onto White Street and continues to the center of town (Mile 610), after which the road becomes South White Street. Just south of this, 21 turns right onto Spratt Street, which quickly takes the route out of town; just over a mile later, the road rejoins the modern bypass.

Known as Cherry Road from this point south, 21 soon crosses the Catawba River, which makes up Lake Norman in North Carolina. Here, it is continuing southeast where it drains into the Wateree River, and later the Santee River, which then drains into the Atlantic Ocean north of Charleston. After crossing the river, the road enters a commercial district on the outskirts of the city of Rock Hill, the state's fourth-largest city with a popu-

Postcard from the Andrew Jackson Court, part of the Quality Courts chain (known as Quality Inns since 1972), circa 1960. It was located two miles north of Rock Hill.

104

(left) Tillman Hall, built by a labor force of convicts in 1894, is a central point on the Winthrop University campus and is on the National Register of Historic Places; (right) Byrnes Auditorium was built in 1939; (below right) Stewart House was built in 1895; All three buildings face Oakland Avenue (Business Route 21).

lation of more than 67,000. It then crosses under I-77 again at Exit 82 before continuing toward town. Just past this, the road comes to another split, with Business 21 going straight through Rock Hill, and Bypass 21 turning left onto North Anderson Road (which it shares with state Route 121, traveling from here west to the Georgia state line). This bypass, traveling east of the town for a roughly five-mile stretch of unremarkable and mostly commercial territory before reconnecting to Business 21, opened in 1950. Business 21 continues west through a very commercial area and into town, passing the entrance to the Winthrop Coliseum, a 6,100 seat arena used by the nearby Winthrop University basketball team. Less than a mile past this, the route turns left onto Oakland Avenue, where it also intersects state Routes 274, which travels several miles north to the state line, and 322, which travels twenty miles into western York County. This intersection is at the edge of the campus of Winthrop University, a highly rated school founded in 1886 and offering numerous degree programs for nearly 6,300 students. Business 21 travels for several blocks through the campus before continuing south; several blocks later it passes over state Route 122, a short road that travels from here east to the interstate. 21 then continues into the historic central district of town when it crosses Main Street (Mile 618). Oakland Avenue ends one block later at East Black Street, where Business 21 then turns left to run in conjunction with state Route 5, which travels between the towns of Van Wyck and Blacksburg. Two blocks east on Black Street, the modern route continues straight, while the original alignment of 21 turned right on Saluda Street to travel south through Chester and then to Ridgeway. This original alignment was changed to the current course in 1950, at

(above left) Porter's Motel, just north of Rock Hill, as seen in the 1950s; (left) The U.S. 21 Truck Stop, as seen in the 1960s, was three miles north of Rock Hill, and boasted of being "South Carolina's Most Modern" truck stop.

105

(left) The Town House Motel, seen in the 1960s, was located at 503 East Main Street, but is no longer standing; (below left) Modern routing of Route 21 through Rock Hill; (right) Built in 1926, the Andrew Jackson Hotel was located on the northeastern corner of Oakland and Main Streets in the center of town; it remains standing today as the Guardian Building.

the same time that the 21 Bypass was opened. The new routing followed an improved and modernized version of what had previously been state Route 5 to Ridgeway.

Following the modern routing first, 21 follows Black Street east for a mile through a mostly residential area before turning left

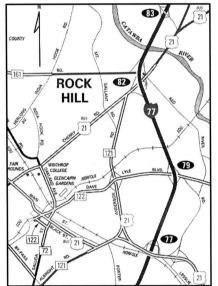

onto Albright Road. One block later this joins East Main Street and continues east with that name. From 1950 through 1962, Business 21 was routed on Main Street from the center of town to this point; from 1962 to the mid-1980s, the route was split, being one-way westbound on Main Street and one-way eastbound on Black Street. From the mid-1980s through the present, the alignment was shifted entirely to Black Street, which reverted to a two-way road. Continuing east away from town, after another half-mile, Business and Bypass 21 reconnect; a brief connector known as Cowan Road takes southbound traffic from the bypass to the business route, and northbound traffic from the business route to the bypass. Eastbound traffic continues on South Anderson Road, quickly crossing over I-77 at Exit 77 before curving south as a four-lane highway. Just past the interstate, Lesslie Highway veers to the right (south); this represents a previous alignment of 21, traveling four miles parallel to the modern road and passing through the census-designated-place of Lesslie, which has a population of nearly 2,300 despite not having a "downtown" district. It then passes through the unincorporated locality of Roddey before reconnecting to South Anderson Road. After passing through another locality known as Harmony, the road enters Chester County (Mile 629), at which point it is renamed as Catawba River Road.

The road continues through a sparsely populated area that is a combination of farmland and dense woods, passing through the localities of Rowell and Landsford; the latter is at the junction with state Route 223, traveling west several miles to Richburg. At this same intersection is an long-abandoned gas station/general store from the road's early days, with a characteristic canopy and pillars on its front side. Catawba River Road

The popular Wagon Wheel Restaurant in Fort Lawn as seen in the early 1960s; it remains in business today with a large addition in the front. Old Route 21 is in the foreground but has since been bypassed by its modern version just to the east, with part of the old road having become incorporated into the restaurant's parking lot.

then continues through the locality of Fudges before reaching the town of Fort Lawn, with its population of 864. The town is most notable for the intersection with state Route 9 (Mile 638), which traverses the entire state from North Myrtle Beach west to the North Carolina state line near Spartanburg. The junction between the two roads is a modern interchange with entrance and exit ramps, and the original alignment of Route 21 (Boundary Road) runs on the west side of the modern road for a mile through this area. The main portion of the town lies just to the west of the intersection, and at the immediate southwest corner of the intersection is the Wagon Wheel Restaurant, one of the area's most popular sites for more than fifty years. This stands across the road from the Holiday Motel of Fort Lawn, which opened around the same time.

Continuing south, the next eight miles of 21 run parallel to the Catawba River, which is directly on the east side of the road. Through most of this stretch, the river forms the lengthy Fishing Creek Reservoir due to being dammed at its southern end. The road is largely unremarkable through this area although in a few places there are good views of the reservoir. Catawba River Road ends at the intersection with state Routes 97 (which connects the towns of Camden and Kings Creek) and 200 (which travels from Winnsboro northeast to the North Carolina state line near Lancaster). Turning left (east) on this road and traveling for a quarter-mile takes one across a bridge where the Fishing Creek Dam can

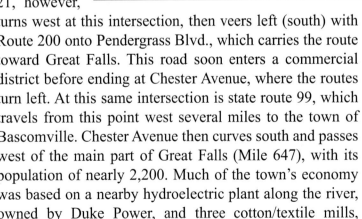

easily be seen. Route 21, however, turns west at this intersection, then veers left (south) with Route 200 onto Pendergrass Blvd., which carries the route toward Great Falls. This road soon enters a commercial district before ending at Chester Avenue, where the routes turn left. At this same intersection is state route 99, which travels from this point west several miles to the town of Bascomville. Chester Avenue then curves south and passes west of the main part of Great Falls (Mile 647), with its population of nearly 2,200. Much of the town's economy was based on a nearby hydroelectric plant along the river, owned by Duke Power, and three cotton/textile mills,

(top right) The Duke Motel, pictured in 1955, was two miles south of Great Falls; **(above right)** Pictured in the early 1960s, the Star Dust Motel was built on the other side of the Duke Motel's restaurant and remains in business today; **(left)** Typical views of the long, straight segments of 21 south of Great Falls. Much of this territory is surrounded by forests, and miles can go by without seeing a single building, or for that matter another vehicle.

(left) The decrepit Carolina Fried Chicken sign is a well-known landmark just south of Great Falls, at the site of the former restaurant, which although closed for years, remains standing today; (below) The First Presbyterian Church, built in 1926, stands at the southwest corner of Main and Saluda Streets in Rock Hill, where the original alignment of Route 21 turned south.

although these are no longer operating. With Route 21 bypassing most of the town, it quickly returns to a rural setting heading south, and two miles later it passes into Fairfield County, at which point Route 200 splits off to head west.

After crossing the county line, the route is renamed as Ridgeway Road. Over the next sixteen miles to Ridgeway, the few scattered houses along the road gradually become more and more sparse before disappearing altogether as 21 travels through one of the most desolate and isolated (not to mention straight as an arrow) stretches along its entire length. The road being surrounded mostly by forest, there is very little to distinguish one mile from another, aside from one crossroads known as Flint Hill, which appears to consist of little more than an abandoned gas station. Finally, as it approaches the town of Ridgeway, a small but pleasant town with numerous Nineteenth-Century southern-style homes and a population of 328, the route is renamed as Palmer Street. Crossing Church Street at the center of town (Mile 665), the road is joined by state Route 34, which crosses much of the state between the towns of Dillon and Greenwood. It also represents a portion of Route 21's original alignment west to Winnsboro.

Returning to Rock Hill to follow that original alignment, Route 21 initially turned south from East Main Street onto Saluda Street to head out of town. Today most of this street has been renumbered as state Route 72, which travels southwest to Chester and then to the Georgia state line. As the road reaches the outskirts of town, it briefly joins state Route 901, which travels from the northwestern side of Rock Hill south and parallel to I-77 for nearly forty miles. Shortly after this, the road is joined by state Route 121, which continues with Route 72 on Old 21 to Chester. Saluda Road then continues away from town, passing the Rock Hill Country Club and several developments of new homes in what was formerly rural territory, as the area has seen continued growth in recent years. After the road passes over Fishing Creek and Stony Fork Creek (both tributaries of the Catawba River), it reaches an intersection with state Route 324, which travels several miles west to the city of York. The road then continues through increasingly rural and unremarkable territory before crossing into Chester County.

Three miles further south, Saluda Road passes through the locality of Lewis, where it is crossed by state Route 909, traveling several miles through rural northern Chester County. Another six miles pass before the road comes to the J.A.Cochran Bypass, carrying state Routes 72, 97, and 121 around Chester. Passing this, the road enters Chester by way of Eureka Mill, a census-designated-place with a population of more than 1,700. Saluda Street then continues through a combination of commercial and residential districts as it nears downtown Chester, the county seat, with its

(top left) Chester County Courthouse in the 1960s; (middle left) Central Chester, looking north on Saluda Street from Columbia Street; the district has a cannon and a Civil War monument, is surrounded by century-old buildings, and is on the National Register of Historic Places; (bottom left) The Chester City Hall and Opera House was built in 1891 and stands at the southwest corner of Saluda and Columbia Streets; it also is on the National Register of Historic Places.

population of nearly 6,500. Upon reaching the central part of town, the road passes the Chester County courthouse, built in 1852, as well as several other century-old buildings before reaching the intersection with Business U.S. Route 321, crossing here on its trek from Lenoir City, TN. to Hardeeville, SC. Route 321 is a spur of Route 21, and until 1950 this was its southern endpoint, with 21 continuing south from here on Columbia Street. When 21 was realigned to the east in that year, 321 was extended south through Columbia to its current endpoint. At this point, the road also intersects state Route 9, which was previously described. At the southwest corner of this intersection is the impressive Chester city hall, built in 1891. Turning left onto Columbia Street, 321/Old 21 gradually works its way out of town, at which point it crosses the J.A.Cochran Bypass, which in this area also carries a bypass version of Route 321 around the town.

After leaving the town, Columbia Road briefly carries state Route 97 (previously described, it heads east to Great Falls) before reverting to a rural setting as it heads south. After passing through the locality of Evans, a segment of the route's original alignment, known as Old Columbia Road, veers to the east, reconnecting to the road a mile later. The road then passes through the locality of Cornwell, and three miles later another segment of the original route, known as Blackstock Road, veers to the east and through the unincorporated community of Blackstock before reconnecting to the main road two miles further south. In the process, the road enters into Fairfield County. The road then continues through the localities of Woodward, White Oak, and Adger before reaching the outskirts of Winnsboro, the county seat, twenty-six miles south of Chester.

On the north side of Winnsboro, Bypass 321 (built in the early 1950s) cuts to the west of town, traveling four miles through an unremarkable mix of rural and commercial territory before reconnecting to Business 321, which represents the

Postcard from the 1940s for the Meade Villa tourist courts near Winnsboro

(left) Fairfield County Courthouse, built in 1823, on Congress Street in Winnsboro; (below right) The Town Clock, built in the 1820s on the site of a duck pond, stands across the street from the courthouse, and was modeled on Philadelphia's Independence Hall. The clock has been running continuously for more than a century, the longest-running clock in the country; (below left) Fairfield County Museum, built in the early 1800s as a private home, stands further south on the west side of Congress Street.

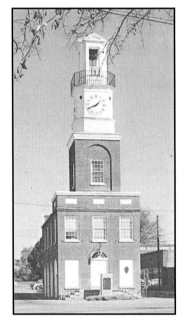

original course of 321 and of course, Route 21. Meanwhile, Business 321 continues into town as North Congress Street, crossing state Route 200 (previously described) in the process. The road then enters the town, laid out in 1785 and originally known as Winnsborough. Today its population is around 3,600 and its central district along Congress Street retains much of its early Nineteenth Century charm. The road passes the county courthouse and a tower known as the "Town Clock" before continuing south and out of town several blocks later. It soon enters the area known as Winnsboro Mills, a mostly residential census-designated-place with a population of more than 2,200. The road quickly passes through the community and comes to the junction with the 321 Bypass before continuing south to Columbia. The

original alignment of Route 21 (Columbia Road) continues south for a half-mile before connecting to state Route 34, which carries Old 21 east for nine miles to Ridgeway. This stretch is extremely rural and the road parallels a railway for its entire length. After passing through the localities of Rockton and Simpson, the road crosses under I-77 at Exit 34 before continuing to Ridgeway.

Upon reaching the town, a bypass of Ridgeway, known as the U.S. 21 Connector, veers south of town for two miles, while state Route 34, which still represents the original course of 21, heads into town as North Dogwood Avenue. It then takes a left (north) on West Church Street, crossing the railroad tracks and then reaching modern U.S. 21 at South Palmer Street, where the route turns right (southeast). Shortly thereafter, the route bears to the right onto South Means Street when it splits from Route 34.

(right) At the northeast corner of Palmer and Church Streets in Ridgeway, where Old and Modern Route 21 meet, the Thomas Company occupies this building. Founded as a general store in 1885, the company moved into the current building in 1911 and remains in business today. The upstairs operates separately as Laura's Tea Room. The building's exterior retains old signs for S&H Green Stamps and Philco radios and appliances.

(right) Two postcards showing the Coronet Motel, at 6320 North Main Street in Columbia, in the 1960s; the motel remains in business with the same name today; (bottom right) The Glass Manor Motel, at 5810 North Main Street, circa 1950; with its ten rooms, it also remains in business today, with the same sign (now thoroughly aged) in front.

Means Street then joins the U.S. 21 Connector and continues south out of town as Route 21. Four miles south of town, after passing through the locality of Smallwood, the road passes into Richland County, the state's second most populous county.

Once in Richland County, the road becomes known as Wilson Blvd. and soon passes through the locality of Boney. Several more miles of unremarkable rural territory pass before the road enters the town of Blythewood (Mile 671), with its population of 170. Known as Main Street during its brief time in the town, the route quickly passes through and continues south. Two miles later, Wilson Blvd. intersects state Route 555, which travels from this point south into Columbia. Another mile further south, 21 crosses under I-77 at Exit 24. After several more miles of rural territory, the road passes Lake Elizabeth, around which is an upscale housing development. This is part of the census-designated-place known as Dentsville, one of the northernmost suburbs of Columbia, with a population of 13,000. Several miles later, the road passes over Interstate 20, which travels more than 1,500 miles from Florence, SC. to Kent, TX. Beyond this, Wilson Blvd. enters the city of Columbia and is renamed as North Main Street. Columbia is the county seat and the state capitol, the second one that Route 21 passes through (Charleston, WV. being the other), and with a population of more than 127,000, it is the state's largest city.

Over the next two miles, the road passes through a combination of commercial and residential areas before reaching the junction with U.S. Route 321 (Fairfield Road), coming south from Winnsboro as previously described. North Main Street carries both routes south from here into downtown. Immediately after this intersection, the road passes Columbia College, a liberal arts Methodist women's college, founded in 1854. Two dormitory buildings face Main Street, with the rest of the campus standing a block to the east. Several blocks later, the road passes the intersection with state Route 215, which runs nearly 100 miles from this point north to Spartanburg. Several blocks further

Aerial view of Columbia College in the 1930s; Route 21 ran past the top left side of the picture. The central brick building remains today, while most of the other structures are gone.

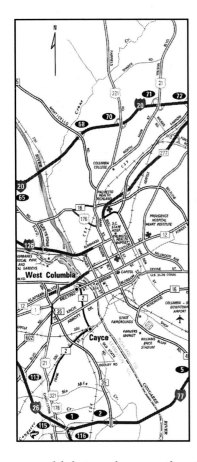

(left) Modern alignment of U.S. 21 can be followed on this current map of Columbia; (above) Current skyline looking north [taken by Ron Wright]; (right) Aerial view of the city, circa 1950s.

south, the road crosses state Route 16, which runs nearly ten miles through greater Columbia. Several more blocks pass before the road is joined by U.S. Route 176, which travels more than 200 miles from Goose Creek, SC. to Hendersonville, NC. The three U.S. highways then continue together into town on Main Street. Several blocks later, the three routes reach Elmwood Street, where they turn right (south) to bypass the

downtown area. The original alignment of 21 continued on Main Street to the statehouse and will be described later. Upon turning on Elmwood Street, the routes are joined by a fourth route: U.S. 76, which travels more than 500 miles from Wrightsville Beach, NC. at the Atlantic Ocean west

(above right) View looking south on Main Street toward the state house, which is dwarfed by the seventeen-story Bank of America Plaza in the foreground, also on Main Street; while Route 21 originally continued on Main to the statehouse, its modern alignment runs several blocks to the west and south of it, with this being the best view of the building from the route; (left) Looking north on Main from the statehouse; the Carolina Life Insurance building in the right foreground remains standing today, as does the red brick Republic Bank Building in the distance; the Wade Hampton Hotel building in the left foreground is no longer standing; (right) View looking south on Main Street in the 1960s, when it still carried Route 21.

to Chattanooga, TN. After following Elmwood Street for six blocks west, Route 76 splits to travel with Interstate 126, which starts at this point and travels several miles west to connect to Interstate 26 west of the city. The other three routes turn left to continue south on Huger Street, traveling parallel to the Congaree River. Five blocks later, the road crosses state Route 12, which travels nearly thirty miles from West Columbia east to Interstate 20. Two blocks further south, the road crosses Gervais Street, which carries U.S. Routes 1 and 378 from the city west across the river. U.S. 1 is a major eastern highway which travels more than 2,300 miles from the Canadian border in northern Maine south along the Atlantic coast to Key West, FL. U.S. 378 travels more than 200 miles from Conway, SC. west to Washington, GA. Six blocks further south on Huger

Street, Routes 21, 176, and 321 turn right (west) onto Blossom Street, continuing across the Congaree River and into Lexington County. At this point, the road also enters the town of Cayce (Mile 691), with its population of more than 12,000, where the road is renamed as Knox Abbott Drive. The Congaree River is formed by the Broad and Saluda Rivers, and eventually drains into the Santee River, which ends at the Atlantic Ocean near Georgetown, SC. Nearly two miles further west on Knox Abbot, the road ends and the three routes turn left (south) on Charleston Highway as they continue out of town. Just prior to this intersection, the road crosses state Route 35, which travels for just six miles through the southern and western parts of greater Columbia.

Going back now to the intersection of Main and Elmwood Streets in Columbia, the original alignment of Route 21 continued south on Main, through the city's central business district at the time, all the way to the statehouse at Gervais Street (Mile 687). Here it turned right (west) to travel with Routes 1 and 378 across the river on the Gervais Street Bridge, an ornate structure that opened in 1928 and is

(above left) The eighteen-story Palmetto Building stands at the northeast corner of Main (Old 21) and Washington Streets. Built in 1913, it is listed on the National Register of Historic Places and has recently been converted into a Sheraton Hotel; across the street from it is the Republic National Bank Building, built in 1924 and also owned and utilized by the Sheraton Hotel; (above right) The South Carolina statehouse, at Main and Gervais Streets, is a Greek Revival Structure that was built between 1855 and 1907 (progress was slowed by both the Civil War and the subsequent Reconstruction Period), and is also listed on the National Register of Historic Places as well as being listed as a National Historic Landmark; (left) The Gervais Street Bridge, opened in 1928, just after the founding of the U.S. Highway System, carried Route 21 until 1954. It is also on the National Register of Historic Places [photo by Ron Wright].

(left) Built in 1968, the Carolina Coliseum stands on Assembly Street and for many years hosted South Carolina Gamecocks basketball games. It remains the home of the Columbia Inferno minor league hockey team today; (below) The Strom Thurmond Wellness and Fitness Center, a relatively new addition to campus, stands at the southwest corner of Assembly and Blossom Streets.

on the National Register of Historic Places. Upon crossing the river and into Lexington County, the road is renamed as Meeting Street and enters West Columbia, with its population of more than 13,000. Route 378 soon veers to the right to continue west out of the city, and Route 1 splits off to continue west a mile later. Old 21 bears to the left at this point, as the road turns into Charleston Highway, connecting to modern Route 21 a mile south of this. This align-

ment of 21 through the city has changed three times over the years; the first change came around 1940, when the route was moved one block west onto the wider Assembly Street for the nine-block stretch between Elmwood and Gervais Streets. Today this is state Route 48, which runs from this point south to the town of Wateree. At that time, 21 still turned onto Gervais to travel across the river. Around 1954, the route was again altered, extending further south on Assembly Street to Blossom Street, then turning west and crossing the river on its current bridge (which was new at the time) into Cayce. For the twenty-four years that the route followed this alignment, it traveled through the southern edge of the main campus of the University of South Carolina. The University was founded in 1801, and has an enrollment of more than 28,000 students, with the Columbia campus covering almost 360 acres of the city. While Route 21 never went through the main part of campus, it did pass the Carolina Coliseum, a 12,400-seat arena for basketball and hockey that for many years was the home to South Carolina basketball teams. In 1978, the route was altered again to its current alignment, running six blocks west of

(top left) West Columbia Trailer Sales stood at the intersection of Routes 1 and 21 in West Columbia until 1954, when 21 was rerouted to the south of this on Knox Abbott Drive; (middle/bottom left) The Tremont Motel, as seen in the 1960s, stood at 111 Knox Abbott Drive just west of the Congaree River bridge; it remains in business today as the Riverside Inn.

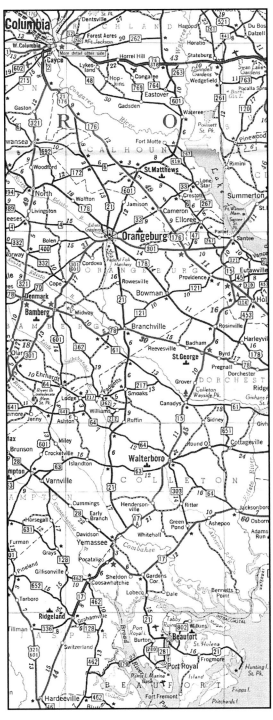

Assembly Street on Huger Street, then turning west on Blossom to cross the river and leave the city.

There are also two brief segments in Columbia today that appear on maps as "21 Connector" (although the actual roads are not marked as such). The first connects U.S. Routes 76 and 378 on the east side of town with current Route 21, running on Devine Street from Millwood Avenue west to Saluda Avenue, where it then connects to Blossom Street and travels through the University of South Carolina campus. It ends after two and a half miles at the intersection with Modern 21 at Huger Street. The westernmost six blocks of this route were part of Route 21 between 1954 and 1978. The other segment connects U.S. Route 1 to Route 21 west of the city, covering a one-mile stretch of Charleston Highway between Meeting Street and Knox Abbott Drive. This was originally a portion of 21 until around 1954.

Going back to the modern routing, once on Charleston Highway going south out of Cayce, the road works its way south through a commercial area, crossing state Route 302 along the way (as it travels more than sixty miles from this point west into Aiken County). At this intersection is Maurice's Bar-B-Q Restaurant, legendary in the region for its menu as well as the Confederate decor inside. A mile south of this, on the east side of the road, are the remains of the Columbia Speedway. Opening in 1948, the racetrack was one of the main sites on the NASCAR racing circuit from 1951 to 1971, although the track had closed by the mid-1970s and has sat largely unused since that time. The road then continues past another intersection with state

Route 2 before passing through the locality of Kinsler. Soon after this, it reaches an intersection with Interstate 26 (at Exit 115), which travels more than 300 miles from Kingsport, TN. to Charleston, SC. Immediately beyond this is Fish Hatchery Road, and turning left (east) upon this takes one directly onto the southern origin of Interstate 77. Route 21 has traveled parallel to I-77 from

(right) Maurice's Bar-B-Q is a notable landmark in West Columbia, as is its huge lighted sign.

its northern origin all the way to this point, which is technically still in the city of Cayce (the interstate covers 610 miles from Cleveland, OH. to this point, while Route 21 has covered 697 miles). While construction of some sections of I-77 in Ohio had started as early as the 1940s, this final section at the south end was not completed until 1995.

Continuing south, Charleston Highway passes through the unincorporated community of Dixiana as the commercial area gradually becomes more rural and sparsely populated. Two miles south of the I-77 junction, Charleston Highway bears to the left with Routes 21 and 176, while Route 321 bears right and continues to the southeast. Two miles past this, the road again crosses over I-26 at Exit 119. Immediately beyond this, the road cuts directly to the right (south) to run parallel to the interstate for approximately two more miles before curving away from it. This stretch was built in the late 1960s to replace a two-mile segment of the route that became part of the grounds of a huge factory operated by the Carolina Eastman Company, a division of Eastman Kodak that opened in 1968 for the production of polyester fibers and yarn. This original section of Route 21 is closed to the public by a gate just beyond the interstate junction, and it is named K Avenue as it passes through the plant. It then reconnects to the modern road on the south end of the plant. The modern route passes into Calhoun County while on this realigned stretch, at which point it is renamed as Old State Road. Six miles into Calhoun County, the road reaches the locality of Sandy Run, where the two routes split; Route 21 bears right onto Columbia Road, while Route 176 bears left on Old State Road, which is an original alignment of 21 to St. Matthews that will be covered later.

The next twenty-two miles to outer Orangeburg are fairly unremarkable. Two miles after the split, the road passes briefly back into Lexington County at the locality of Oak Grove. Another mile brings it back to I-26, which it crosses over at Exit 129. Two more miles bring the road back into Calhoun County, and four miles after that comes an intersection with state Route 6, which travels 160 miles from Richland County to Berkeley County. Soon after this is an intersection with state Route 172, which travels nine miles west from this point into Orangeburg County. At this point, 21 runs parallel and a half-mile to the west of I-26 for several miles. Five miles further to the south, the road passes into Orangeburg County, and over the next seven miles, the area gradually becomes more populated as the road draws near the city of Orangeburg. The seat of Orangeburg County, the town was originally settled in 1704 and was named after William IV, the European Prince of Orange. Known as The Garden City, it has a population of more than 13,000 and lies along a branch of the Edisto River.

Upon reaching the outskirts of Orangeburg, Route 21 turns left (east) on Chestnut Street, which it shares with U.S. Route 178, (traveling more than 200 miles from Dorchester, S.C. to Rosman, N.C.). After a mile on Chestnut Street, the road crosses Magnolia Street NE, which carries Business Route 21 into town, along with U.S. Route 601, which travels more than 300 miles from Mount Airy, N.C. to southern South Carolina. Modern Route 21 continues to circle the eastern side of the city, bypassing downtown as Chestnut Street and later as Whittaker Parkway, which also carries

1940s view of Russell Street in downtown Orangeburg, looking north from near Broughton Street (which would later be Business Route 21 for several years).

bypass Routes 178 and 601. The road then passes the edge of South Carolina State University, a historically African-American college founded in 1896 and with an enrollment of nearly 5,000 students. Most of the campus lies to the west and is not visible from the highway, with the exception of the Oliver C. Dawson football stadium, with a capacity of 22,000. Continuing south, the road crosses state Route 33, which travels from downtown Orangeburg east to Lone Star in Calhoun County. Another mile south brings the road to an intersection with U.S. Route 301, which travels 1,100 miles from Sarasota, FL. to Glasgow, DE. Beyond this, Route 21 is known as the Joe S. Jeffords Highway, and after two more miles, the route again meets Business 21, which ends here after coming out of the town; Route 21 then turns left (south) on Rowesville Road to continue south.

Meanwhile, Business 21 follows an original segment of 21 through the town, running for

nearly three miles along Magnolia Street. As it parallels a main line of railroad tracks on the north end of town, it passes the western edge of Claflin College, founded in 1869 as another historically African-American school. With an enrollment of 1,800 students, the small institution lies adjacent to South Carolina State University. Just past the college, the road passes state Route 33, also known as Russell Street. This is the main street going through the downtown district (Mile 728), which lies just to the west of Business 21. South of this, the road passes through a mainly residential area before passing the county fairgrounds on the east side. Less than a mile south of this, the route turns left onto Charleston Highway, as it briefly meets up again with U.S. Route 178. It then quickly turns right onto Rowesville Road, ending just after this at the junction with Modern Route 21.

The course of Route 21 around the Orangeburg area has changed twice over the years, in conjunction with the route being removed from the town of St. Matthews, so we now return to the locality of Sandy Run, where the original alignment of 21 continued southeast on Old State Road, or modern U.S. Route 176. The fifteen mile trip to St. Matthews is entirely unremarkable, aside from passing through the locality of Hammond Crossroads. Upon nearing St. Matthews, original Route 21 cut east on West Bridge Street (modern state Route 6), taking it three miles into the center of town. St. Matthews is the Calhoun County seat, with a population of just over 2,100. Upon reaching the junction with U.S. Route 601, today known as Harry C. Raysor Drive, original Route 21 turned right (south) to quickly head south and out of town. By the mid-1940s, a bypass had been created around the town such that Route 21 continued on Old State Road instead of turning onto West Bridge Street. It connected to modern Route 601 approximately two miles south of town at the locality of Wertz Crossroads, where 21 then turned south and continued to Orangeburg as St. Matthews Road. The thirteen mile drive to Orangeburg is largely unremarkable; the road passes through the localities of Riley and then Jamison at the Orangeburg County line, and several miles later crosses over I-26. It then passes through the locality of Stilton as it approaches the north-eastern outskirts of Orangeburg, eventually connecting with modern Route 21 when St. Matthews Road becomes Magnolia Street.

Around 1950, Route 21 was realigned entirely away from St. Matthews, following its modern course along Columbia Road, then southeast on Chestnut Street and south on Magnolia (modern Business 21) into and through town. At that time, the original Business Route 21 was created, continuing south on Columbia Road. Over the next two miles, the territory gradually transitions from commercial to residential before the road ends at Park Street, turning right for one block before turning left (southeast) on Broughton Street, which today carries Business Route 178. Over several blocks, the road gradually leaves the residential neighborhood and enters the downtown district, centering around Russell Street (state Route 33). Two blocks later, the road crosses U.S. Routes 301 and 601, and several more blocks take the road out of downtown and back to the junction of Magnolia Street and Charleston Highway, where the route continued south and onto Rowesville Road to leave Orangeburg. In the mid-1960s, the modern bypass on the town's east side was completed, with the main route's alignment moving onto that, as it remains today. At that time, the original Business 21 routing was eliminated, with the traditional Magnolia Street alignment becoming Business 21, as it also remains today.

Leaving Orangeburg on Rowesville Road, 21 travels through mostly rural territory over the next seven miles. Along the way it passes through the locality of Felder, where the road has a brief stretch as a four-lane divided highway, with a half-mile stretch of the original alignment visible just to the left (east) of the road. It then reaches the town of Rowesville, with its population of 378 (Mile 736). Modern 21 travels just to the east of the town, with the original alignment veering to the right (west) of the road just north of town as Calhoun Street. This goes through the center of the small town and continues south, approximately one mile west of Modern 21, for the eight miles to Branchville, where it reconnects to the current road in the center of town. Meanwhile, Modern 21 passes Rowesville and becomes known as Freedom Road, passing through the locality of Sixty-Six and mostly farmland over the next eight miles.

Upon reaching Branchville, first settled in the 1730s and with a population today of nearly 1,100, the road first intersects state Route 210, which travels from this point east for nearly thirty miles to the village of Vance. In the center of town (Mile 744), it crosses U.S. Route 78, traveling more than 700 miles from Charleston, S.C. to Memphis, TN. At this point, the road crosses a main line of railroad tracks which have been in place since the 1830s. One of the first railroad lines in the country, the line went from Charleston to near Augusta, GA., follow-

The Branchville Railroad Shrine and Museum, located at 7204 Freedom Road (Route 21), is located in the old town depot in the center of town. It stands at the site of the oldest railroad junction in the country, built in 1842.

BRANCHVILLE - OLDEST RAILROAD JUNCTION

Inside the Branchville Railroad Shrine and Museum, there is a scale model of the "Best Friend of Charleston," the original steam locomotive that traveled along the railroad between Charleston and Augusta, through Branchville.

ing a previously existing Indian trail. In 1842, a branch line was opened, going north from Branchville to Columbia, and this was considered to be the world's first railroad junction. Today, the town depot stands along Route 21 and is used as a railroad museum, with the historic junction located directly across the street.

Leaving Branchville, Freedom Road continues south for five miles through a very sparsely populated mix of forest and farmland before crossing the South Fork of the Edisto River (Mile 749), which travels southeast from here to the Atlantic Ocean, where it ends at Edisto Island. The river also forms the border of Bamberg County; Route 21 passes through a tiny slice of this before entering Colleton County just a half-mile further south. At about the same point, known as Whetstone Crossroads, the road crosses state Route 61, which travels from rural Bamberg County to Charleston. South of this, the road is known as Low Country Highway. Six miles further south, the road passes through the small town of Smoaks (Mile 755), with its population of 140. This lies at the intersection with state Route 217, which travels approximately fifteen miles through rural Colleton County. Just north of Smoaks is a brief segment of the road's original alignment, known as Garris Hill Loop, which travels for a half-mile just west of the modern road. Another six miles brings the road through the locality of Ruffin (Mile 761). Two more miles brings the road to Bells Crossroads, at the intersection with state Route 64, which travels more than seventy miles from Jacksonboro to the Savannah River. Another six miles south is the locality of Sniders Crossroads (Mile 770), at the intersection with state Route 63, traveling nearly thirty miles from Walterboro to Varnville. Two 1930s-era gas stations, one still operating as Buddy's Stop & Shop, the other long-abandoned, are about all that exists today in Sniders.

Another ten miles pass before the road intersects Interstate 95 at Exit 42. Built in this area in the 1970s, I-95 is the primary highway along the East Coast, traveling more than 1,900 miles from the Canadian border with Maine to Miami, FL. Just past the exit is the small village of Jonesville, and a mile past this is the intersection with U.S. Route 17-A, or Alternate. Route 17 is another major East Coast highway, traveling nearly 1,200 miles from Winchester, VA. to Punta Gorda, FL., and it is the main coast road throughout the Carolinas and Georgia. In southern South Carolina, an alternate version of Route 17 appeared in the early 1950s, traveling more than 120 miles from Georgetown to Pocotaligo, and it is this segment, known as Hendersonville Highway, that 21 intersects. In the original 1926 alignment, this was the southern endpoint of U.S. 21, with its total length being 793 miles. As originally drawn, the route would have continued along U.S. 17 to Jacksonville, FL., making it a true "Lakes-to-Florida Highway," but for unknown reasons the route ended here when it was actually put in place. In 1935 the route was then extended further south to Beaufort and in 1954 further east to Hunting Island. From the junction with Route 17-A, Route 21 turns right to travel with 17-A for the next seven miles. Less than two miles beyond the junction, the road crosses the

Early postcard showing Lane's Cabins near Yemassee

119

Salkehatchie River, which drains into the Combahee River, which then drains into the Coosaw River, which empties into St. Helena Sound and the Atlantic Ocean east of Beaufort. The Salkehatchie River forms the line with Hampton County, which the road enters at that point.

Two miles into Hampton County, the road reaches the town of Yemassee (Mile 786), with its population of just over 800. Yemassee is in the center of the region known as the Low Country, a loosely defined area that includes several counties in the southernmost section of the state, includ-

ing the towns of Beaufort and Hilton Head. By some definitions it includes areas as far north as Charleston, primarily along the Atlantic coast. The sights of Palmetto trees (the state symbol) and Spanish moss are common throughout this area. The region was first settled by Europeans in the late 1600s, although the area around Yemassee was designated as "Indian Lands," for use by the Yamasee tribe for which the town was named. This

ended after Yamasee War of 1715, after which the tribe left the area. The area also has sites that were part of the Revolutionary and Civil Wars. Despite the history, there is not a lot to see of the town from Route 21, which passes through quickly and continues southwest. The original alignment of 21 turns left (south) on Yemassee Highway in the center of town, and less than a mile later passes the town's Amtrak station before crossing the main line of railroad tracks through the area. It then travels as Castle Hall Road for another mile and a half before intersecting modern Route 21, where it continues as

(right) The Gardens Corner Restaurant and Motor Hotel, as seen in the 1960s; in the pre-Interstate era, chain motels were not commonly seen in smaller towns, and numerous privately owned motels and motor courts often stood near junctions of major U.S. highways; (middle right) Esso gas station and the Gardenia Restaurant that operated adjacent to the motel, as seen in the 1940s [courtesy of Joe Bartolini, whose parents operated the restaurant during that era]; (below right) View of the restaurant after being remodeled in the 1950s; this and the gas station remained standing until 2008, when they were razed for the rebuilding of the intersection. The motel had been razed some years earlier.

Castle Hall Road. Meanwhile, the modern routing travels directly out of town for a mile before crossing the same railroad tracks, at which point the route enters Beaufort County and is renamed as Frampton Road. This soon intersects Castle Hall Road and continues south for another two miles to the junction with U.S. Route 17, at which point 17-A ends. This is on the edge of the locality known as Pocotaligo, which was originally an Indian town; most of it lies west of 21 along Route 17. From here, 21 and 17 continue south together as Trask Parkway, a four-lane divided highway. Though not particularly scenic, the parkway forms a modern and direct route from I-95 to Beaufort and the surrounding area.

Seven miles further along, the road comes to the locality of Gardens Corner (Mile 796), at the junction where 21 continues east to Beaufort and 17 continues northeast to Charleston (this intersection is currently being completely rebuilt as shown below). Along the way, the road crosses Huspa Creek, a tributary of the previously mentioned Coosaw River. Also at Gardens Corner, Old Sheldon Church Road turns left (north), heading back to Yemassee. Less than a mile along this road are the ruins of Old Sheldon Church, also known as the Prince William Parish Church. Built between 1745 and 1759 with solid brick walls, the church was burned by British troops in 1779. After being rebuilt years later, it was again burned by General William Sherman's troops in 1865 during their "March To The Sea," which effectively crippled the Confederacy and brought a quick end to the Civil

(above left) Aerial view of Gardens Corner as it appeared for many years, with Routes 17 and 21 coming from the north in the upper left, and Route 21 continuing south at the bottom; the motel and restaurant stood at the triangle in the center; (left) Diagram of the intersection as it will appear when completely rebuilt in 2011; the unique layout will include a roundabout for traffic coming north from Beaufort.

(right) Although the Highway 21 Drive In Theater sign is along Route 21, the theater itself is actually a quarter-mile west of the highway along Parker Drive, near the Beaufort Marine Corps Air Station.

War. The walls and columns of the church remain standing today, and ghost stories are often told about the site. Beyond Gardens Corner, Route 21 continues south through the locality of Lobeco before crossing the J. V. Dunbar, Sr. Memorial Bridge over the Whale Branch River, which empties into the Coosaw River and eventually into St. Helena Sound.

At this point, Trask Parkway has crossed onto Port Royal Island, which includes the towns of Beaufort and Port Royal. This is part of the Sea Island region, consisting of over 100 low-lying coastal islands from South Carolina to Florida, all of which are separated by a series of rivers. Once on the island, the road passes through the community of Seabrook, and three miles later the locality of Grays Hill (Mile 805). Just past this, the road passes on the west side of the Beaufort Marine Corps Air Station, a huge military airfield covering nearly 7,000 acres that was established in 1943. Also known as Merritt Field, it is home to

around 4,000 members of the military that are stationed there, and is also home to all East Coast-based F/A-18 fighter jet operations. While the airfield is not visible from Route 21, several military air-

(above left) Several military aircraft are displayed along Route 21 at the entrance to the Beaufort Marine Corps Air Station; (above) The Blue Angels in formation at an air show held at the Air Station; (left) Aerial view, looking east, of the Air Station in the foreground, with Route 21 seen on its right side; this view shows the entire island area, with Hunting and Fripp Islands and the end of 21 in the distance [Copyright John M. Hudson; used with permission].

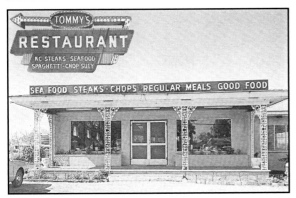

(left) Three postcards from the 1940s through the early 1970s, showing Coclin's Motor Court, which was located near the gateway to Parris Island; due to several changes in ownership over the years, the associated restaurant went from Mrs. Coclin's Kitchen to the Lobster House and later Tommy's Restaurant. The motel and restaurant are no longer in operation.

craft are displayed outside its entrance. This is at the intersection with state Route 116, which travels west from here to Laurel Bay, where many members of the military are housed. While access to the airbase is normally restricted, it hosts occasional airshows which are open to the public.

A mile past the airbase, the road intersects state Route 280, also known as Parris Island Gateway. It travels four miles south to the entrance to the Parris Island Marine Corps Recruit Depot, where new members of the Marines have gone for initial training since 1915. Roughly 17,000 recruits go to Parris Island each year. Beyond Route 280, the road enters the city of Beaufort, with its population of nearly 13,000, after which the road becomes known as Boundary Street. Founded in 1711, the city is the second-oldest in the state, behind only Charleston, and is the Beaufort County seat. It is one of the most picturesque towns in the South due to its historic setting and abundant antebellum architecture, and has been the site for filming numerous movies, such as *Forrest Gump* and *The Big Chill*. After another mile through a commercial district, the road intersects state Route 170, which travels west nearly forty miles to the Georgia state line. Another mile east brings the road to an intersection with Ribaut Road, which takes a right (south) here. This is Bypass Route 21, formed in 1989 to replace

(right) Some of the thousands of graves at the Beaufort National Cemetery, many of which lie underneath old stately trees in a sterotypical Southern setting.

(right) Beaufort College building, built in 1852, stands on the east side of Carteret Street as part of today's University of South Carolina Beaufort; (below left) The university's performing arts center, also on Carteret Street, was used in the filming of the movie *Forrest Gump*, where it was temporarily renamed as the Gump Medical Center.

former state Route 281; its course will be covered later. Meanwhile, going straight on Boundary Street is Business Route 21, which was the original course of the route after it was extended to Beaufort in 1935. Two blocks past the intersection, the Beaufort National Cemetery stands on the north side of Boundary Street. Listed on the National Register of Historic Places, the cemetery was established in 1861 for burial of Union troops who died in the area during the Civil War. It has had military burials from every major U.S. conflict since that time, and currently has nearly 19,000 graves. Continuing past the cemetery, the road begins to enter the older part of town, and eight blocks later it ends at an inlet of the Beaufort River. This point is known as Bellamy Curve, and Route 21 then turns right (south) onto Carteret Street, which takes it into the downtown district.

At this point the route has entered into the Beaufort Historic District, which includes much of the town and features numerous homes and businesses with various styles of antebellum archi-

tecture. The district is on the National Register of Historic Places and is designated as a National Historic Landmark. Once on Carteret Street, the route passes through the University of South Carolina Beaufort, one of three campuses in the University of South Carolina system. The school opened in 1959 and has nearly 1,500 undergraduate students. The educational origins at the site go back to 1795 with the founding of Beaufort College, the primary building of which still stands in the center of campus. The college closed at the outset of the Civil War, and the building was used as a Union Hospital and later as an elementary school. It was incorporated into the newly opened university in 1959, and the campus has seen steady growth since that time. Across the road from this is the original St. Peter's Catholic Church, built in 1846, and the small church cemetery behind it. The building is still used as a chapel, although the congregation now uses a modern building on Lady's Island. Several blocks further south, the road comes to the intersection with Bay Street (Mile 813) at the center of town. From 1935 to 1954, this was the southern endpoint of U.S. 21, with state Route 285 continuing south across the Beaufort River and then further east as a relatively unimproved road. In 1954, the road to the ocean had been completed through the swampy lowlands, and finally received the U.S. highway designation all the way to its current endpoint on Hunting Island, replacing the state route designation.

Aerial view of downtown Beaufort, showing the approach to the Woods Memorial Bridge over the Beaufort River

124

Bridge between Port Royal Island and Ladies Island.

(left) Two views of the original Beaufort–St. Helena Bridge that crossed the Beaufort River from 1927 to 1971; its approach was made primarily of wood; (below) Two views of the current Woods Bridge, built in 1971; its approach is built entirely of concrete and steel.

After crossing Bay Street, the road is renamed as Sea Island Parkway and enters onto the ramp to the Woods Memorial Bridge which crosses the Beaufort River. Named after Richard V. Woods, a state highway patrolman who was killed in the line of duty, it was built in 1971 to replace the original Beaufort–St. Helena Bridge that was built in 1927. The Beaufort River is part of the Atlantic Intra-

coastal Waterway, and therefore has a significant amount of marine traffic; therefore both spans have been built as swing bridges to allow the larger vessels to pass. This created occasional problems with traffic congestion in Beaufort until the 21 Bypass was established in the late 1980s, taking much of the through traffic out of the downtown area. The entire length of the Woods bridge, including the north and south approaches, is approximately a half-mile. The bridge was another site used for the filming of *Forrest Gump*, in a scene where Forrest is being interviewed while

crossing the bridge as part of a cross-country run. Just beyond the bridge's southern end, White Hall Drive veers to the west and then briefly parallels the approach to the bridge; this is the only remaining portion of the original road and approach to the old bridge. Once beyond the bridge, the road has reached Lady's Island and the locality of Hazel Farm. It then passes the Lady's Island

Lady's Island
South Carolina

Marina, along the Beaufort River. This entire area has traditionally had a rural feel to it, but in recent years it has been developed significantly with both commercial and expensive residential properties. Currently, Ladys Island has a population of more than 12,000, similar to the town of Beaufort itself. At the center of the Ladys Island community, Business 21 reconnects to Bypass 21, known as Ladys Island Drive, and also designated as state Route 802.

Ladys Island Marina, just east of Business Route 21

(left) Beaufort County Courthouse on Ribaut Road;
(below left) Current routing of 21 through/around Beaufort;
(below right) Sea Island area and the J. E. McTeer Bridge
taking Bypass 21 across the Beaufort River to Ladys Island.

Following Bypass 21 now, the route begins west of Beaufort at the intersection of Boundary and Ribaut Roads. Following Ribaut Road south, it almost immediately passes the modern Beaufort County Courthouse complex before continuing three miles south through a mostly residential area along the Beaufort River toward the town of Port Royal, with its population of more than 9,000. First settled as a French colony in 1562, the main part of town is largely bypassed by modern Route 21, which soon turns left to head east toward Ladys Island.

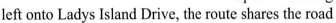

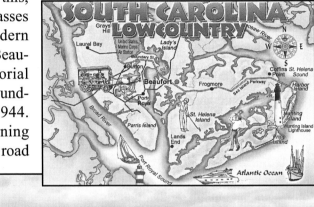

Just before this, the road passes the modern five-story Beaufort Memorial Hospital, founded in 1944. Upon turning left onto Ladys Island Drive, the route shares the road with state Route 802, which travels sixteen miles from the Broad River to the Coosaw River, all in the Sea Island region. The road quickly reaches the J. E. McTeer Bridge, a 2,200 foot span which crosses the Beaufort River and is named after a longtime former sheriff of Beaufort County. Built in 1981, the bridge is significantly taller and wider than the Woods Bridge in Beaufort, and therefore does

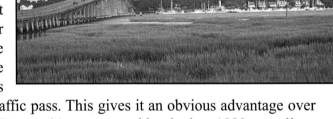

not require a moving segment to let marine traffic pass. This gives it an obvious advantage over the Woods bridge and is the main reason that Bypass 21 was created by the late 1980s to relieve some of the traffic flow in downtown and minimize the frequent traffic backups. Despite the fears

of many merchants in downtown, the bypass has not ruined businesses in that area. Currently, there are plans to build a second span parallel to the McTeer Bridge, with each becoming one-way, to improve traffic flow even more. Once on Ladys Island, the road continues another two miles before reaching Business 21, at which point the bypass ends and Route 21 continues east.

Less than a mile further to the east, the road

Beaufort County Airport on Ladys Island
(photo provided by Sy Commanday)

126

(left) Shrimp boats are a common sight in the waters surrounding the Sea Island region through which Route 21 passes; (below) The general store in Frogmore, on Route 21 and built around 1900, was originally the headquarters of the MacDonald Wilkins Company, an area cotton dealer.

passes just south of the Beaufort County Airport, also known as the Frogmore Intranational Airport. With one runway, the field averages around 100 flights per day, most of its traffic consisting of single-engine planes. Two miles further east, the road crosses Cowen Creek and onto St. Helena Island (Mile 817). The eastbound end of this small bridge (which has been rebuilt and widened in recent years) was another site used in the filming of *Forrest Gump*, in a scene where Forrest is running cross-country; at this point he was seen entering the state of Mississippi (with a large sign indicating this erected along the road for filming purposes; it is no longer standing). Two more miles through primarily rural territory brings the road to the unincorporated village at the center of the island, known variously as St. Helena or more commonly as Frogmore. Named after an

FROGMORE, SOUTH CAROLINA

Eighteenth-Century plantation on the south side of the island (which in turn was named after an English estate), Frogmore consists of a few small businesses, a general store, and the Gullah Grub restaurant. The Gullah culture is a group of African-Americans who live throughout the Low-country region, with a particular concentration on St. Helena Island. They are descended from slaves that had originally been taken primarily from Sierra Leone and Liberia in Western Africa as far back as the early 1700s to work on nearby rice plantations. Due to geographic isolation in the Sea Island area and other historical factors in the post-Civil War era, this particular group is thought to have preserved more of its original African cultural heritage and language than any other African-American group in the United States. Many of those living in the Sea Island region are self-sufficient with farming or fishing and a relatively simple lifestyle to this day, as they have

(above) Gullah Grub Restaurant in Frogmore; (right) Gay Fish Company and its dock along the Harbor River at the eastern end of St. Helena Island.

127

done for generations. This area is also known for the origin of Frogmore Stew, also known as Beaufort Stew, a Gullah dish which consists of fresh shrimp, corn, sausage, and potatoes.

Continuing east, the road passes a small rusted sign advertising Sunbeam Bread and the 21 Open Air Market, which appears to have seen better days long ago. A little further, the road passes the St. Helena Prayer Chapel, a tiny building in the shape of a church. Beyond Frogmore, the area becomes more sparsely populated, and the road crosses Village Creek after another two miles. The easternmost three miles of the island are a fairly unremarkable mix of small farms, forests, wetlands, and occasional homes, until the road reaches a marshy area leading up to the Harbor River. Here stands the Shrimp Shack Restaurant, as well as the Gay Fish Company with its multiple fishing boats, where fresh jumbo shrimp, grouper, tuna, and other local fish can be bought at the small market inside. The road then crosses the Harbor River, which travels along the

Old Hunting Island Lighthouse, 1859.

southern end of St. Helena Island and empties into St. Helena Sound. A swing bridge (pictured in the introduction of this book) is at the center of this crossing, allowing the many local fishing vessels to pass. Beyond the bridge, Sea Island Parkway reaches Harbor Island (Mile 827), one of the smaller sea islands, that is primarily made up of a portion of Hunting Island State Park and beachfront homes. Here the road begins a long gradual curve to head south, parallel to the ocean, to its endpoint. One of the few

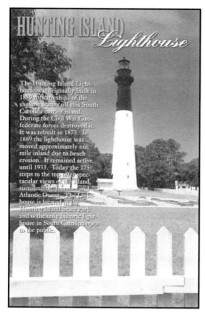

HUNTING ISLAND *Lighthouse*

The Hunting Island Lighthouse was originally built in 1859 to warn ships of the shallow waters off this South Carolina barrier island. During the Civil War Confederate forces destroyed it. It was rebuilt in 1873. In 1889 the lighthouse was moved approximately one mile inland due to beach erosion. It remained active until 1933. Today the 175 steps to the top offer spectacular views of the island, surrounding marshes, and Atlantic Ocean. The Lighthouse is located in the Hunting Island State Park and is the only historic lighthouse in South Carolina open to the public.

(left) Modern view of the lighthouse; (top right) View looking up the inside of the lighthouse; (below right) Views from the top of the lighthouse, looking north, south, and east, respectively.

commercial establishments on Harbor Island is the Johnson Creek Tavern, located just north of Johnson Creek, which separates Harbor and Hunting Islands.

Upon crossing the creek and onto Hunting Island, the end of Route 21 is almost in sight. The island is covered entirely with forest and marshland, and makes up the majority of the Hunting Island State Park. One of the island's interior inlets was the site of filming some of the Vietnam scenes in *Forrest Gump*. The exact endpoint of Route 21, however, is somewhat debatable, and while it has changed at least once since the route was extended to the island in 1954, it appears differently from one map to the next. Some maps indicate that although Sea Island Parkway extends the entire length of the island, the U.S. Highway designation ends at the north end of the island. Based on the posted signs along the road, it appears that the current official end point is at the entrance to the state park, also known as Hunting Island Drive, roughly at the midpoint of the island (Mile 831). South of this point, the road continues to the south end of the island as state Route 406. However, at least one map suggests that 21 continues with Route 406 to the south end of the island, where

the road crosses the Fripp Inlet to Fripp Island. Yet another map suggests that Route 21 continues on Fripp Island, where it is known as

(left) View near the base of the lighthouse, looking toward the beach; the gap in the trees [also seen in the above photo] was the original path of Route 21, although the pavement is gone from this area.

(left) Two close views of the lighthouse; (right) View from the beach.

Tarpon Blvd., to the south end of that island. This potential endpoint is not supported by any other findings, however. Historically, the original routing of 21 took it along a curved road (now closed off), a mile north of the park's current entrance, eastward to the ocean, at the site of the Hunting Island lighthouse. It then turned south, running parallel to the modern road and the beach, for approximately two miles before it ended at the south end of the island. At that time, the beach was several hundred feet further east than it is now, and there were trees and buildings on both sides of the road. In 1980 this alignment was abandoned due to extensive and ongoing erosion of the beach, which had damaged the roadway. This pavement from this older alignment ends today just northwest of the lighthouse, and the original beach road is no longer in existence.

Hunting Island was originally used by the area's earliest settlers for hunting its vast array of wildlife. It was also a popular layover spot for eighteenth century sailors and pirates, including Edward Teach, also known as Blackbeard the Pirate. The state park was built in the 1930s by the Civilian Conservation Corps. It covers 5,000 acres and has three miles of beach with showers and dressing rooms, as well as a campground, rental beach cabins, marsh boardwalk, nature trails, lagoon, fishing pier, and a boat landing. With more than a million visitors annually, it is one of the most popular state parks in South Carolina. The beach has been subject to severe erosion over the years due to the combination of ocean currents and high tides, and additional sand has been brought in on several occasions to replenish it, along with steel reinforcements and boulders. It was this erosion that caused the rerouting of Route 21 from the beach inland.

The most notable feature of the park is its lighthouse, the only traditional one in the state with public access. The island's first lighthouse was 95 feet tall and built of brick in 1859, but was destroyed in 1861 by Confederates during the Civil War, so that the Union Army that had taken control of the area would not be able to use the light. The current structure was

(right) Entrance to Fripp Island and its beach

Fripp Island — Fabulous resort Island on the Atlantic Ocean.

(left/below) Two more views of Fripp Island and its beach; (bottom right) Aerial view of the southern end of Tarpon Blvd. on Fripp Island, which purists might argue to be a more logical true endpoint for Route 21.

built at a cost of $102,000 between 1873 and 1875 on the north end of the island, although due to erosion at that site, the building was disassembled and moved by rail line (at a cost of $51,000) to its current location more than a mile to the south in 1889. Interestingly, the building was built of cast-iron segments that could be taken apart if necessary, indicating that the builders anticipated the erosion problem from the beginning. Standing 136 feet tall, the top is accessible via 167 wrought iron steps, and a narrow exterior walkway gives one a remarkable view of the island and the ocean (although it is not recommended for those with a fear of heights). When in operation, the light was visible for seventeen miles out to sea, although the station was deactivated in 1933. The park currently maintains a light in the tower at night, although it is not used for navigational purposes. The site is on the National Register of Historic Places.

While Route 21 officially ends on Hunting Island, the road does continue south, as mentioned previously, crossing Fripp Inlet to Fripp Island where it encounters an entry gate. This is a private island with nearly 900 year-round residents, and access is limited to those who own or rent property there. It was largely undeveloped prior to the bridge from Hunting Island being built in 1961. Like Hunting Island and Beaufort,

it has been used in the filming of several Hollywood movies, including *The Prince of Tides*. Today there are many oceanfront homes along the three miles of beach and two golf courses on the island, and it is a popular vacation destination for those seeking a quiet spot near the water. Once on the island, the road becomes Tarpon Blvd., and it continues three miles to the south end of the island where it ends in a cul-de-sac by Skull Creek. While this is not the official southern endpoint of Route 21, it is definitely the end of the journey, nearly 840 miles from its beginning in Cleveland.

Well, there you have it...the entire road covered in 130 or so pages. While this may not be the easiest book to sit and read, it is intended more as a travel companion for anyone who wishes to take on the challenge of following Route 21, either in total or even a short stretch on a Sunday drive. I can only hope that they find it as entertaining as I have over the past forty years.

Summary of Mileage

Cleveland, OH	0	Mount Hope	332
Independence	10	Beckley	339
Brecksville	15	Ghent	354
Richfield	21	Spanishburg	370
Montrose	28	Princeton	380
Copley	31	Bluefield	393
Loyal Oak	34	East River Mountain	398
Clinton	43	Rocky Gap, VA	404
Canal Fulton	46	Bland	417
Massillon	55	Big Walker Mountain	426
Navarre	61	Wytheville	440
Strasburg	70	Independence	469
Dover	76	VA/NC state line	473
New Philadelphia	78	Sparta, NC	479
Stone Creek	88	Roaring Gap	496
Newcomerstown	98	Elkin	510
Cambridge	122	Harmony	531
Byesville	128	Statesville	547
Ava	139	Troutman	552
Belle Valley	143	Mooresville	562
Caldwell	148	Davidson	569
Dexter City	155	Huntersville	576
Marietta	180	Charlotte	590
Williamstown, WV	181	Pineville	601
Vienna	190	NC/SC state line	602
Parkersburg	195	Fort Mill, SC	610
Mineralwells	201	Rock Hill	618
Rockport	210	Fort Lawn	638
Ripley	232	Great Falls	647
Fairplain	237	Ridgeway	665
Sissonville	255	Blythewood	671
Guthrie	264	Columbia	687
Charleston	270	Cayce	691
Belle	280	Orangeburg	728
Glasgow	289	Rowesville	736
Smithers	297	Branchville	744
Gauley Bridge	307	Smoaks	755
Chimney Corner	311	Yemassee	786
Fayetteville	319	Beaufort	813
Oak Hill	325	Hunting Island State Park	831

* The original length (in 1954) of U.S. 21 was officially listed at 843 miles; the mileages shown here are based on my own experience with the modern road, which has been rerouted from its original alignments, cutting the total length slightly.